SUSAN WILSON

EXPLORE HALIBURTON

PHOTOGRAPHY BY MICHAEL SHIRLEY

Enjoy Exploring!

Susan Wilson

Stoddart A Boston Mills Press Book

Wilson, Susan, 1944-
    Explore Haliburton

Includes bibliographical references.
ISBN 1-55046-134-6

1. Haliburton (Ont. : County) - Guidebooks.
2. Haliburton (Ont. : County) - History.
I. Shirley, Michael, 1946-   . II. Title.

FC3095.H35W55 1995   917.13'61044   C95-930793-1
F1059.H27W55 1995

Book design and typesetting
Chris McCorkindale and Sue Breen
McCorkindale Advertising & Design

Printed in Canada

First published in 1997 by
The Boston Mills Press
132 Main Street
Erin, Ontario, Canada
N0B 1T0
519-833-2407 fax 833-2195

An affiliate of
Stoddart Publishing Co. Limited
34 Lesmill Road
North York, Ontario, Canada
M3B 2T6

Front cover:
Davis Barn, Blairhampton

Title page:
Gull Lake circa 1930
Photo courtesy Carol Moffatt

Back cover:
Hawk River Falls

The publisher gratefully acknowledges
the support of the Canada Council, Ontario
Arts Council and Ontario Publishing Centre
in the development of writing and
publishing in Canada.

CONTENTS

To all the people of the Haliburton Highlands

who have shared their stories with us,

and especially to

Jack Brezina,

who first gave us the chance to relate them.

FOREWORD

As you drive north from Norland along Highway 35, a mile or more of unwaveringly straight flat road leads towards the Haliburton County line. A moment after you cross the county line, the road drops down a hill and goes around a corner. For me, that moment, and that change of terrain, sum up the essence of the Haliburton Highlands and elicit an irrefutable sense of arrival, no matter how much longer my journey.

That moment is all the more extraordinary when you realize that this line, like all county and township boundaries, was drawn arbitrarily over a century ago by men in offices with rulers and pencils, to be confirmed later by surveyors with rods and transits. It is a remarkable congruence of geography and geometry. But, however straight these boundaries appear on paper, this countryside is not so docile as to be forced into any mapmaker's strait-jacket.

Haliburton County marks the southernmost edge of the Precambrian Shield. The hard but beautiful landscape is the ice-scoured consequence of the glaciers that retreated 10,000 years ago, leaving behind the long-fingered lakes and the grey and rose outcroppings of granite. Together with the lonely windswept pines, these make up the scenes that, thanks to the Group of Seven and other artists, hold such a central place in the Canadian psyche.

The Haliburton Highlands are neither flat nor straight, and the roads here have been forced out of the Victorian

For many years, this moose was a welcome landmark after the long drive up from the city. The sign marked the Haliburton County line on Highway 35 north of Norland and indicated that journey's end was not far ahead. Photo courtesy John Hulbig.

conformity common among concession roads to the south by the immovable reality of the lakes. This makes exploring Haliburton an endless adventure in what's around the corner. It might be an expanse of shining water, a dramatic rock cut, or a vista sweeping to the far hills.

Exploring Haliburton is also an adventure in retracing history. The major highways approximate the routes of the original colonization roads, built in the mid-19th century to encourage the movement of settlers away from the overcrowded Front (as the counties bordering Lake Ontario were known) and into the back country. This coincides, happily, with my preference for looking at the world through a historical prism. It's an intriguing exercise of the imagination, for instance, to contemplate heading up these roads (sans pavement) in an oxcart laden with all one's worldly possessions, children of various ages perched on top, travelling into an unknown wilderness to start life over on an uncleared homestead.

But the forces of "progress" are always straightening out the curves in highways, speeding us into the future and leaving aside the places people built on what were once the main roads. And that raises the second personal bias that informs these pages: my penchant for back roads, especially if I'm not quite sure where they go. So this book will encourage you to get off the main road now and then to discover what time has left behind. I've never come a cropper while taking a chance on an unknown byway, and you have my assurance that every back road I suggest is one I can vouch for.

There are many ways to explore Haliburton. This book concentrates on exploring it by car. Ten tours are offered, beginning with Minden in the southwest corner and working east and north. Each tour is accompanied by a large map that shows the whole route of that tour. In some cases, there are also smaller maps that show a community in more detail. The numbers in circles on the maps indicate the approximate location of the sites mentioned in the text; the number in the circle corresponds to the number of the heading in that chapter. (The other numbers are highway and county road numbers.) Each tour has been laid out so that you can follow the numbers in order and, except for the three village tours (Chapters 1, 5, and 10), you will end up just about where you started out.

I've also highlighted a few of the many events put on by residents of the county for their own pleasure and amusement, as well as that of cottagers and visitors.

But you can also see Haliburton by canoe, cross-country skis, snowmobile — even shank's mare. Indeed, there are many areas you can't get to by any other means. The final chapter suggests other ways to explore Haliburton.

There is a list of accommodations at the back of the book. Our thanks to these people for supporting the publication of this book.

The natural beauty, the sense of adventure, the feeling of being on the edge of an untamed wilderness have brought visitors to Haliburton for over a century and lured many others to make their homes here. We invite you to come and see for yourself all the things that make Haliburton worth exploring.

ACKNOWLEDGMENTS

Creating a book is a team effort. The author — and in this case, the photographer too — are just the ones with their names on the cover. Behind them stand many other people whose contributions are essential to the finished product you hold in your hand. This book would not have been possible without any of them.

In a rural area such as Haliburton, oral history is the main source of our knowledge of the past. Documented facts can be hard to come by. Fires that destroyed homes and businesses and whole main streets also burned down newspaper offices, sending up in smoke all those irreplaceable back issues. And a hundred years ago, as now, the outside world paid scant attention to what happened here. So there aren't many other places to look.

In Haliburton, we are at a critical stage in our history. The grandchildren of the original settlers are now grandparents themselves. They are the last ones to have heard the family and community stories of a century ago first-hand around the kitchen table. What they have to share is precious and irreplaceable.

So my thanks must go first to the scores of people in Haliburton County and beyond who have invited me into their homes, offered me cups of tea, and generously shared their stories and their knowledge. To present all their names here would leave little room for anything else. I hope that they will take their reward from this sharing with you of what they have shared with me.

But as with any project, there are some people who have contributed more than others and so they deserve to be mentioned by name. The first of these is Jack Brezina, publisher of *The Times*, the weekly newspaper published in Minden.

I'd been a cottager in Haliburton County all my life. But it wasn't until 1988, when Jack invited me to write and edit the summer supplement to *The Times,* that I began to develop what I call a sense of context—an understanding of and appreciation for my surroundings.

I'd never done anything like this before: called up people, gone out to interview them, come back and written up the stories, and then helped get them into print. Jack threw me in at the deep end of the pool and trusted me to learn how to swim. It was an invaluable education — six summers and over 200 articles that formed the basis for this book.

People who have a thirst for history are rare creatures. Those who make the effort to dig it up and share it with others are rarer still. I count among my friends several such people who make their home here. I turned to them frequently in my efforts to make these pages thorough and accurate.

Leopolda Dobrzensky and her family were forced by history to leave their homeland, the Czech Republic, and a centuries-old, aristocratic way of life. After several years, they came to Canada and eventually Leopolda and John retired to an old homestead outside Haliburton village. There she took it upon herself to do months and months of tedious basic research on the early days of the nine townships bought by the Canadian Land and Emigration Company and bring what she learned to light in her own invaluable book, to which I referred frequently. Her example has inspired me and her advice has increased my confidence in those parts of the book that relate to her part of the county.

John Hulbig's maternal and paternal grandparents came to settle in the southern part of the county 125 years ago. As the only child of middle-aged parents whose own parents had been getting on in years when they were born, John has a unique grasp of almost the entire span of the county's history. I find his sense of history and its importance for the future uncommon among people of his time and place. Thank goodness John inherited his mother's love of telling stories and has put them together in his own chronicle.

Tom Ballantine is the closest thing to a professional historian we have. A graduate of Trent University in anthropology, Tom combines his love of history and prehistory in his job as head of the Haliburton Highlands Museum. The museum's holdings are eclectic and as thorough as he can make them.

Ruth Still came from Quebec to Eagle Lake as a seasonal resident several years ago and fell so in love with the place that she retired here. She too became absorbed in the history of her adopted community and has put her indomitable drive and enthusiasm to good use in writing the history of Eagle Lake. Without her ground-breaking work, this section of the book would be much poorer.

Carol Moffatt has taken as her domain Stanhope Township. A third-generation cottager and now a resident, Carol has made collecting the story of Stanhope in words and pictures her personal mission. To this end, she has established Stanhope Heritage Discovery, dedicated to preserving the history of that part of the county. Her own book is just a matter of time.

The Gull River flows through the village of Minden, providing a pleasant recreational spot in the middle of town for swimming, boating, canoeing or just strolling along the riverbank under the willow trees.

Guy Scott of Kinmount and John Clayton of Dorset have been particularly generous with their time, information, and contacts in helping me learn about their communities.

It is to another writer, however, one who doesn't live in Haliburton, that this book owes the critical debt of inspiration. It was Susan Pryke's successful book *Explore Muskoka* that first gave me the idea for a similar book about Haliburton.

Which brings us to Boston Mills Press and its publisher, John Denison, who published Susan's book. John is by nature an energetic and enthusiastic kind of guy, and those are the attributes he demonstrated when I called him out of the blue seven years ago and asked if he'd like a book that explored Haliburton.

There's been a lot of water under the bridge for all of us since I first approached John. I am very grateful to him for maintaining the faith he first showed in the project and for being a survivor in the tough days that Canadian publishing has been going through. Boston Mills has a well-deserved reputation for producing fine books and it is an honour to be in their catalogue.

Behind John is an industrious and committed team. My thanks to the ever-patient managing editor Noel Hudson and his assistant, Kathy Fraser, to editor Sarah Reid (it's bad enough editing writers; how much worse it must have been for her to edit an editor!), and to designers Chris McCorkindale and Sue Breen whose beautiful work makes us all look good.

Finally, these remarks would be incomplete without a word of thanks to my husband, Michael Shirley. This is more than the usual offering of gratitude from a writer to a spouse for faith and forbearance. I thank Michael for getting as excited as I did about the opportunity to create this book and for the care and commitment he showed in taking the photographs.

Writing a book based largely on oral history is fraught with peril. While I have made every effort to ensure the accuracy of what you read here, I accept full responsibility for any errors and omissions. If you find any, I hope you will let me know.

Susan Wilson
Blairhampton, Ontario
December 1996

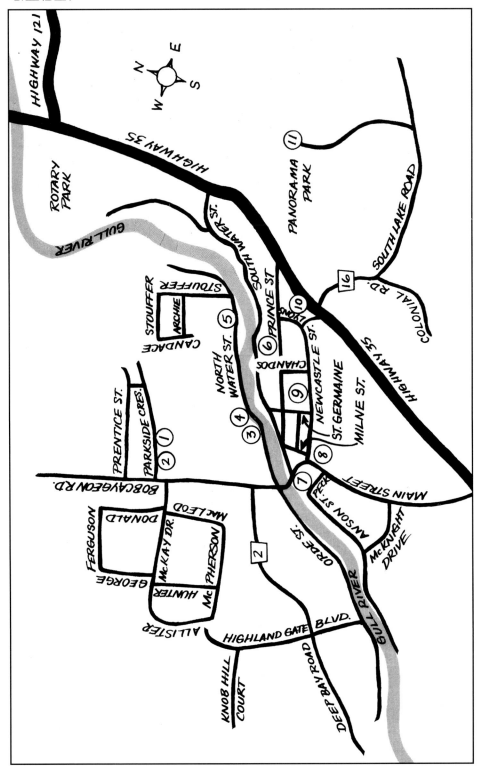

CHAPTER ONE

MINDEN VILLAGE

This township is now being settled with an industrious and intelligent class of people, composed chiefly of immigrants of a few years' experience in the country, who have acquired a good knowledge of Canadian life. There are already several large clearings varying from two to fifteen acres, the greater portion of which is under crop. . .

J.W. Fitzgerald, O.L.S.

When J.W. Fitzgerald arrived in the area in 1858 to begin surveying for the government of Upper Canada, he found a modest commercial centre growing naturally at the junction of two transportation routes: the Gull River and the proposed route of the Bobcaygeon Road. This hamlet bore the name Gull River, after the waterway beside which it was built.

In 1859, the road and the post office both arrived at Gull River. To mark these events, it was decided to change the name of the community. During the Seven Years' War, an alliance of British and German armies had defeated the French in 1759 near the north German town of Minden. Although its importance has faded for us, this had been such a significant victory that even a hundred years later, it was still worthy of great celebration. As part of those celebrations, the government of Upper Canada changed the name of the community to Minden.

Although Fitzgerald had emphasized the farming activities of the area, Minden began as a rough-and-tumble logging town, its origins reflected in the most ungridlike layout of its streets. River drives passed through town annually. Many loggers were the breadwinners of local homesteading families; the money they earned working during the winters in the logging camps supplemented the living they made from farming in the snow-free seasons. It is easy to forget today that it was the women who managed the families and farms and did all the backbreaking labour during those long, cold months when their husbands were gone. The lumbering industry did not survive as a dominant economic force much past the end of the 19th century. After the First World War, summer visitors began to infiltrate the area. Their numbers grew slowly until the cottaging boom took off after the Second World War. Since then, Minden has been the commercial centre for cottagers on the surrounding lakes, some of whose families go back three and four generations on the same lake.

Two postcard views looking north up Minden's Main Street show the differences between the way it looked before and after the fire in 1942, which took out most of the east side. Note the vacant lots as yet unrebuilt in the second picture. The Sterling Bank still stands at the corner (car out front) in the earlier picture. Top photo courtesy Carol Moffatt. Bottom photo courtesy John Hulbig.

The County Town Museum and its historical buildings offer visitors a chance to step back into the area's history and to learn about the people and events that have shaped its growth.

1·MINDEN COUNTY TOWN MUSEUM

The museum is housed in the Sterling Bank building, which was built in 1915 at the corner of Main Street where the Canadian Imperial Bank of Commerce currently stands. The Standard Bank took over in 1920, followed eventually by the CIBC. In 1958, when the bank built a new building, this structure was moved to Peck Street to house the library. When the new library and gallery building opened in 1981 (see No. 2 below), the old bank building was taken over by the museum and moved here in 1984.

Other buildings in the museum's historical village include the Bowron Homestead (which from 1860 to 1988 stood at the corner of Main Street and Highway 35, where the Home Hardware store is now), a replica of the Bethel Church (we'll visit the original later in these pages), and the Hindon School, brought from the long-vanished hamlet of Hindon, farther up the Bobcaygeon Road on the other side of Highway 118. A general store will be added in the near future. During the summer, the museum offers programs for the public and is also the starting point for walking tours of the village.

2·AGNES JAMIESON GALLERY

Agnes Jamieson was a beloved doctor who served this area from 1939 to 1956. Through gas rationing and snowstorms and seven-day workweeks, Jamieson logged over a thousand house calls a year. With her nurses, Sylvia Howard and Olga Myles, who worked with her here and elsewhere for 40 years, she cared for the people of the county. She was instrumental in the establishment of the local hospital and, in 1942, became the first woman in Ontario to be appointed coroner. In 1956, she left Minden to work in Smith's Falls and, later, Orillia. When Jamieson retired in 1972, she returned to Minden with Howard and Myles. An avid oil-painter—and a five-foot-nothing dynamo—she was the guiding force behind the creation of the art gallery.

The building that houses both the gallery that bears her name and the Minden Library opened in 1981. The gallery includes in its permanent collection a number of Jamieson's paintings and 41 works by the renowned artist Andre Lapine. Touring shows and the works of local artists are regularly on exhibit.

3·ST. PAUL'S ANGLICAN CHURCH

St. Paul's Anglican Church is the oldest church structure still in use in the county. Construction is thought to have begun in 1866. The women of the congregation papered the interior with newspapers to cover the cracks and keep out the drafts; a paper from 1871 was uncovered when the parish hall was added in 1947. The pulpit, altar, and pews that serve today's congregation were made by Alf Langdon, a cabinetmaker who, several years before he moved to Minden in 1907, had worked on the counters and fittings in Timothy Eaton's first store in downtown Toronto. The church building remained largely unaltered until 1947, when the tower and parish hall were added.

It should be noted that the historical plaque outside the church is not entirely accurate. This township was not one of those bought by the Canadian Land and Emigration Company. It was in Haliburton village that the company supported a missionary and it was there, at St. George's Anglican Church, that Frederick Burt began his work in this county in mid-1865. He and his wife, Louisa, moved to Minden in November of that year to establish the congregation here.

4 · MINDEN HOUSE

Minden House has been standing almost as long as the town itself and has been home to some of its best-known citizens. Although the early history of the house is not clearly documented, William Watts is generally considered to have built the earliest part of the house not long after he received a Crown grant in 1866. (Watts also donated the quarter-acre of land for St. Paul's.)

The construction of the house is unusual. It was built using the block-house or stacked-timber method, in which undressed boards were placed horizontally on top of each other, each board displaced one inch in or out from the one below. The gaps created by the staggered placement were filled with plaster.

The origins of Minden House date back to the village's earliest days. The elegant and idiosyncratic house has been a tourist home for the past six decades.

In 1884, the house was bought by Michael Brown and his wife, Jane Hawthorne Dunn. Brown was an Englishman who became county treasurer that year; he subsequently served for many years as postmaster and justice of the peace. The Browns are credited with adding a substantial section to the back of the house, along with several touches of elegance and idiosyncrasy, such as oak baseboards and moulded trim around the doorways and windows. Perhaps they were also the ones who installed the handsome front door, with its contrast of white etched-glass and red stained-glass.

Michael Brown died in 1930 and, in 1934, under the ownership of Dick and Laura Kirkwood, Minden House became a tourist home, a role it still plays six decades later.

5 · PHILLIPS HOUSE

The Phillips House is one of the few brick houses in Minden—and probably the only one with three storeys, high ceilings, front and back staircases, oak floors, oak banisters, and 14-inch oak baseboards. When it was built in 1905 by school inspector Sylvanus Phillips, it must have been the talk of the town.

In 1939, Phillips's successor, Archie Stouffer (for whom the local elementary school is named), bought the house and lived there for over 30 years. During Stouffer's tenure as school inspector, the spacious lawn was the regular site of school concerts; the verandah became the stage and the audience sat on chairs on the grass.

6 · THE CLERGY HOUSE

Although the Clergy House is acknowledged to be one of the oldest structures in the county, its origins are wrapped in mystery. One source reports that the log building was put up in 1853 by a man named Dickson as an outpost for the Strickland Lumber Company of Lakefield. Another says it was built in 1870 for the same purpose and, indeed, this is as far back as the Ontario government was prepared to go when it put up the historical plaque on the lawn in 1958. The Stricklands sold it to the Lakefield Lumber Company in 1888; there is some suggestion that these two companies may have been the same operation under different names. In 1890, Lakefield sold the building into private hands.

The house gained its current name in 1899 when it was sold to the Anglican Synod in Toronto and began half a century of service as the rectory for the Anglican mission priests serving the area. It also housed a small chapel where intimate weddings and baptisms were performed. When the house was sold back into private hands in 1949, the furnishings of the little chapel were moved across the river to the baptistry of St. Paul's.

The Clergy House, acknowledged to be one of the oldest structures in the county, is a treasured Minden landmark. For half a century the property of the Anglican church, it is now privately owned.

7 · DOMINION HOTEL

The Dominion Hotel is said by some to be the oldest hostelry in town, but there is precious little documentary evidence to back up the claim. We do know that when James and May Mortimer bought it in 1908 from William McCracken, it was a going concern — and McCracken had bought the land in 1874.

Mildred Mortimer Bath, James and May's daughter, was born at the Dominion Hotel in 1910. A few years ago, at the age of 81, she clearly recalled growing up there:

We had a lot of clients who came up from Toronto and from the States to hunt and fish. They stayed there on their way to the hunt camps because there were no resorts above Minden then.

There were a lot of travelling salesmen too —travellers, we called them. My father had a room set aside where they could display their samples — shoes, dry goods, and so on. The storekeepers would come to the hotel to look over the goods and place their orders. There were three general stores in Minden then: Hartle's, Soward's, and Welch's.

The dining room downstairs was in two sections — one for the travellers and other business people, and one for the farmers, loggers, and labourers, who were not as likely to be so well dressed. The dining room was fully licensed, as was the bar.

In its most recent history, the Dominion has not been a hotel, though everyone still calls it that. Several years ago, a terrible fire at the Inn on the Park in Toronto compelled provincial authorities to come up with stiffer fire regulations for hotels. But, realizing that the cost of bringing small old hotels up to the new code would be prohibitive, they permitted businesses such as the Dominion and the Rockcliffe to close their guest rooms and operate only as drinking and eating establishments.

8 · ROCKCLIFFE TAVERN

The first public house on this site may have been Daniel Buck's legendary but little-documented hostelry of the 1860s, before the Crown deeded the lot into private hands in 1869. The property passed through several hands over the next 40 years, until it was bought by Thomas Ranson in 1908. Ranson House, as he called it, was run by him and his heirs for the next three decades.

The Valley View Inn was one of the earlier incarnations of the Rockcliffe Hotel. Elements of the original architecture can still be seen. Photo courtesy Carol Moffatt.

By 1933, when Lorna Ryan journeyed to Minden by motor car, it was called the Valley View Inn. Ryan wrote of the experience for *Canadian Motorist,* the Ontario Motor League's magazine:

An Inn was a new experience in my life because I had not stayed at a country hostel before. Oil lamps burned in the simple but cleanly bedrooms, and there were coils of brand new rope under each bed. These I was told were to be used in case of fire, but, with a noose on one end, they would be just dandy to hang oneself with.

Spotless rugs swam about on the glassy linoleum everywhere, and there were prints of strawberries and clematis in the dining room.

15

The earliest reference to the establishment as the Rockcliffe Hotel appears in a photograph from 1939, when it was bought by Thomas and Maude Campbell. The self-styled sobriquet "World Famous" dates from the mid-1970s, when then-owner Bill O'Brien decided to sell T-shirts with the pub's name on them. Since then, clothing sporting the tavern's name has been seen around the world. Indeed, it has been called the clothing store that sells beer.

People introduced to the Rockcliffe through the T-shirts often expect something extraordinary when they finally cross the threshold. What they find is a basic but quintessential Northern Ontario bar where friends have gathered for at least a hundred years.

9 · MINDEN UNITED CHURCH

The location of Minden United Church encapsulates in its way the history of the formation of the United Church of Canada. The original Methodist church was the one-storey building at the corner of Newcastle Street and St. Germaine Street; the two-storey white frame building between it and the present church was the Methodist manse. (Both now house a lawyer's offices.)

Across the street stood the Presbyterian church, which later became the Orange Lodge. It burned and was rebuilt in 1937, then later became the Masonic Lodge. The house with the screened verandah immediately to the east of the Masonic Lodge was the Presbyterian parsonage.

Details of the early days of the Methodists in Minden come from the reports of the ministers to church headquarters. Perhaps the first was George Henry Kenney, a circuit rider who arrived in 1860. It is clear from his reports that to be successful in

these parts, a clergyman had to be made of the same tough stuff as his pioneering congregation.

During this year, I preached three times each Sunday except one in four, travelling by bark canoe along rivers and over lakes, footing it through woods and swamps, frequently without as much as a trail. If I got lost, I would keep a lookout for a blaze on the trees and then follow it till I came to a corner stake, observe its number, then on to the next when I could ascertain the course to take. I visited everybody in the country, finding a welcome everywhere and making myself at home everywhere and so finding a lodging place wherever the night overtook me.

The Methodist mission was undeniably a busy one. Minden-based circuit riders were also responsible for Bethany (up Bobcaygeon Road), Gelert, Lutterworth, Snowdon (on the Burnt River), Bethel, Providence (Ingoldsby), Progress (Lochlin), Straffords, and Allsaw (Lake Kashagawigamog).

In 1864 and 1865 respectively, the Free Presbyterians and the Wesleyan Methodists received Crown grants and built houses of worship. In 1918, seven years before formal church union, the Methodist and Presbyterian congregations came together. This pattern was being repeated throughout the county (and, indeed, throughout the country) as rural congregations addressed the problems of low numbers and limited resources. Formal church union on June 26, 1925, which brought together the Methodists, the Congregationalists, and 85 percent of the Presbyterians, was the simple recognition of many faits accomplis.

In 1925, in anticipation of union, the combined Minden congregation decided to build a new church. It was one of the first in the area to be built on contract, instead of by volunteer labour. The contract went to a Mr. Fetterly in Haliburton, who had his own lumberyard. He and the head carpenter, a Mr. Sipe, floated the wood on rafts to the foot of Canning Lake, then hauled it to Minden by team and wagon. The bricklayers came from Lindsay, apparently because there was no one skilled in that trade locally. Alf Langdon built the pews in this church, as he had in St. Paul's Anglican and several others.

Electricity was put into the church in 1936, the same year the Orillia Water, Light, and Power dam just outside town was completed. The chancel was added in 1958.

10 · THE BRICKYARD

The broad, shallow depression behind the houses on the north side of Newcastle Street was the site of Minden's brickyard. The depression was created by quarrying the deposit of clay. Bricks made here were used to build several local homes, including John Dauncey's house on Lake Kashagawigamog (see Chapter 6, No. 3).

11 · PANORAMA PARK

Panorama Park stands on the top of the cliff overlooking the river valley. It offers an ideal vantage point from which to survey the town and is a pleasant spot for a picnic.

EVENTS

The *Timbersports Festival* is held on a Saturday in mid-June. It offers modern-day lumberjacks the chance to compete in ten events for cash and points. The festival takes place right on Main Street, which is closed to traffic for the day.

The *Highlands Artisans Festival* takes place every Canada Day weekend and offers a wide range of arts and crafts

Clifftop Panorama Park offers a sweeping vista over the Gull River valley and the village of Minden.

17

created by artists from the local area and around Ontario.

The *Crazy Raft Race* is a fun-filled feature of Minden's annual Canada Day celebrations. Dozens of rafts, each one decked out in some silly fashion, float through town and under the bridge on the Gull River's steady current.

The *Minden Rotary Carnival* is held on the evening of the last Wednesday in July. It is an alcohol-free event geared to children.

The *Highland Yard* is a 4 1/2-mile rural footrace run each year on the Friday of the long weekend at the beginning of August. Begun in 1972 as a friendly challenge among three counsellors at Camp Onondaga, the Highland Yard has grown into an annual event that attracts over 400 runners and many more spectators. All proceeds from the race are donated to the Amici Camping Charity, which sends children to camps throughout Ontario.

The *Haliburton County Fair*, first held in 1865, takes place annually on the third weekend in August. It offers all the trappings of a country fair, including horse pulls, livestock shows, and a parade through town.

The *Minden Techni-Cal Challenge*, which began in 1985, is the world's largest limited-class speed race for sled dogs. It is held annually in late January and regularly attracts top competitors from across North America. The start-and-finish line on Main Street offers thousands of spectators a ringside view of the action as up to 100 eight-dog and four-dog teams compete for the largest limited-class purse on the continent, donated by Martin Pet Foods. The race is sanctioned by the International Sled Dog Racing Association to ensure the welfare and safety of the dogs.

The Minden Techni-Cal Challenge draws thousands of spectators to the streets of Minden each year to see the world's top mushing athletes—human and canine—compete for the largest limited-class purse on the continent, provided by race sponsor Martin Pet Foods.

CHAPTER TWO

CIRCLE TOUR FROM MINDEN: KINMOUNT, IRONDALE, GELERT

Distance: 65 kilometres (39 miles)

Starting in Minden, this tour follows the routes of two colonization roads and a back-country byway. After heading south down Highway 121 (formerly the Bobcaygeon Road) to Kinmount, the tour continues east along Highway 503 (formerly the Monck Road) to the vanished village of Irondale, then back to Minden via the (almost) ghost town of Gelert.

1 · BOWRON HOMESTEAD

This corner was the site of the homestead established around 1860 by Francis and Mary Bowron. Their original log home, which stood on the spot now occupied by the Home Hardware store, was moved to the Minden County Town Museum's pioneer village in 1988.

In his report for 1866, road agent Richard Hughes reported that the Bowrons were of English origin, that there were 5 people in the family, that in 1865 the Bowrons had 16 acres cleared, none chopped (that is, the stumps were still in the ground), and 11 under crops, with 2 more for pasture. That year, they produced 60 bushels of wheat, 15 of oats, 20 of peas, 350 of turnips, 100 of potatoes, 5 of corn, none of barley, and a ton of hay. They had two oxen, one cow, no calves, sheep, or pigs, and two horses.

Except for the horses, which remained a rare commodity in the county for many years, this was fairly typical. The lumbermen wanted the settlers to grow bulky produce such as hay, oats, turnips, and potatoes, which were expensive to ship. By buying locally, the lumbermen could save on the shipping charges; the settlers, for their part, had a ready cash market. The rest of the settlers' produce and livestock was for their own tables.

2 · S.S. LUTTERWORTH NO. 5

S.S. Lutterworth No. 5 (now partly hidden behind a row of trees) was built in 1878 to replace a small log school that had served the area on the same site since 1863. At the time, it was the only painted school north of Bobcaygeon—red with white trim. Hence its nickname, the Red School.

The building now belongs to John Hulbig, a lifetime resident of Lutterworth Township who went to the school as a boy in the 1930s and, for 14 years starting in 1946, drove the school bus that brought children from the surrounding area to S.S. No. 5. In summer, he drove a 1927 Oldsmobile; in winter, he used a horse-drawn sleigh with a wood-heated cab of his own construction. Since Hulbig bought the school and land and built his own house, he has used the schoolhouse as a workshop and a place to store his collection of historical memorabilia.

3 · HOWLAND JUNCTION

Howland Junction was named for Henry S. Howland, son-in-law of Charles J. Pusey, who founded Irondale. Howland was involved in Pusey's iron-mining ventures and helped establish the I.B.&O. Railway in 1884 to ship out the ore from his father-in-law's mines at Irondale.

The I.B.&O. was originally intended to go from Irondale to Bancroft and on

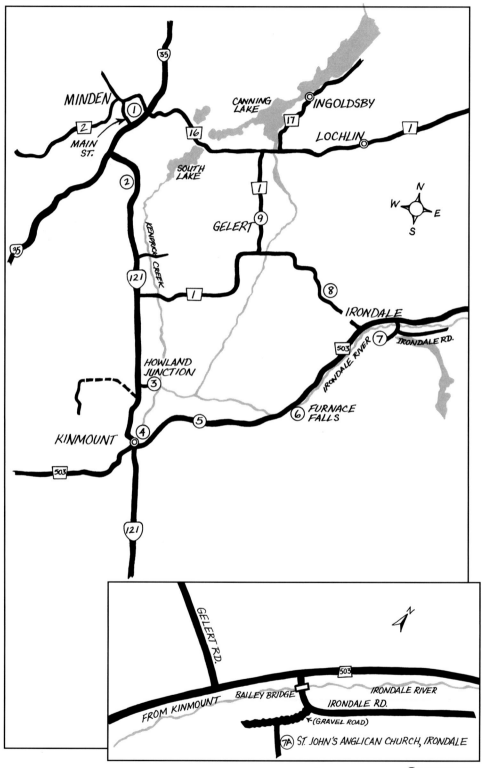

to Ottawa—hence the initials. But it never reached its intended destination; indeed, the first train didn't even get to Bancroft until 1910. The last I.B.&O. train passed this way on March 31, 1960. The rails were torn up shortly afterwards and sold to a razor-blade company. The corridor now serves primarily as a snowmobile trail.

At Howland Junction stood the turntable that linked the Victoria Railway (completed in 1878) to the I.B.&O. Locomotives were driven onto the turntable and the wooden platform was turned by hand to change the direction of the locomotives. The wide, round, shallow hole that once housed the turntable now stands on private land at the end of Howland Junction Road.

4 · KINMOUNT

The village of Kinmount grew at the junction of the Burnt River and two colonization roads: the Bobcaygeon Road and the Monck Road. With the arrival of the Victoria Railway in 1876, the town became a prosperous transportation hub for the area. At one time, there were five sawmills operating on the river. Stores sprouted along the main street to serve rising expectations. The railway brought in more settlers and took their produce out to the world.

Kinmount was subjected to four "Great Fires." The first, in 1890, destroyed 13 businesses. But afterwards, as the old photographs testify, Kinmount sprang like a phoenix from the ashes to a new magnificence. In 1898, five businesses were burned out; only the efforts of bucket brigades kept the blaze from spreading.

The town's prosperity continued until 1917, when fire gutted five businesses on the east side of Main Street. Insurance coverage was not enough to match the losses; so rebuilding on the same scale was not possible. The economy deteriorated further after the First World War, when the loggers and the farmers moved from the land they had exhausted to greener fields out west.

The fourth fire, in 1942, started in the piles of sawdust at Austin's Mill. The firestorm spread so quickly through the wooden buildings that people were hard pressed to save even their personal possessions. One man just locked the door of his store and walked away as the flames did their work. The only survivor was the old railway station. This time,

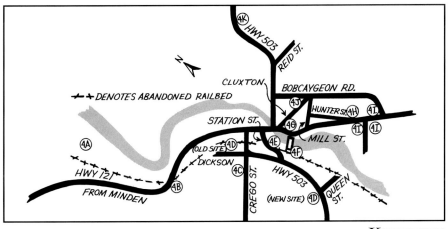

· KINMOUNT

21

there was no supporting economy and the townspeople rebuilt once again on a still smaller scale.

4A · KINMOUNT STAVE FACTORY

This was originally the site of a shingle mill built by Alexander McIntosh in 1880. McIntosh sold his operation to R.J. Mills in 1883; a year later, it burned to the ground. Mills rebuilt immediately and expanded the business to include railroad ties and barrel staves. Henceforth the site was known as the Stave Factory.

At its peak, 50 employees worked in a complex spread along the river bank. Every week, the steam-powered mill dispatched a railway car filled with its wood products along its own railway siding.

One of the original locomotives of the Victoria Railway Company steams across the high trestle bridge over Kendrick's Creek, north of Kinmount. The Victoria Railway brought to four the number of transportation routes that met in Kinmount. The others were the Burnt River, the Bobcaygeon Road, and the Monck Road. Photo courtesy Guy Scott.

However, the Stave Factory was constantly plagued by financial problems and it passed through the hands of many owners. It closed in the 1930s, another victim of those cruel economic times, and the structures disappeared one by one. All that remains are the bunkerlike concrete kilns where the staves were steamed and bent into shape for the barrels they would eventually become.

4B · HIGHLANDS CINEMA

The Highlands Cinema was established in 1979 by film buff Keith Stata. In the lobby of his movie house, he has also created a widely renowned museum of old projectors, including one from the Royal Alexandra Theatre in Toronto and another from composer Irving Berlin's home.

Stata has also rescued an amazing array of memorabilia from over 300 demolished movie houses, from Prince Edward Island to Victoria, British Columbia, to furnish and decorate his four small theatres. Everything, from the theatre seats to the toilet seats, has been rescued from somewhere else.

4C · ST. JAMES ANGLICAN CHURCH

The increase in local population sparked by the Victoria Railway led the Anglican Rural Dean in Lindsay to form a parish in the area. A mission was set up in Kinmount and the Rev. Phillip Tocque was appointed to the post. Judging from Guy Scott's description of Tocque in *History of Kinmount: A Community on the Fringe*, he was hardly suited to the realities of a pioneering community. "Reverend Tocque wore a long swallow-tailed coat and was an eccentric, intellectual type who seemed out of place in rough, frontier Kinmount. Evidently, this mission did not agree with the Reverend for he left about 1878, minus some back stipend."

Tocque was replaced in 1882 by Edward Soward, who would remain for the next quarter-century. Like all his contemporaries, Soward preached in lumber shanties, schoolhouses, and homes, and travelled over the wagon and lumber trails of the region, usually on foot. He continued the practice, even

St. James Anglican Church was built in 1883 under the direction of the minister, Edward Soward, who served the congregation until 1907.

in his later years when he was reportedly blind, following the railway tracks south to Burnt River and east to Irondale.

In the village itself, Soward, like Tocque before him, held services in the Presbyterian church. Apparently this amicable ecumenical arrangement faltered one spring day in 1883 when the Anglicans arrived to find the Presbyterian church locked. The agreement was abruptly terminated and the Anglicans promptly formed a committee to build their own church.

Other versions of the story suggest, however, that plans to build an Anglican church in Kinmount began soon after Soward's arrival in 1882. In any event, as was customary, the structure was built with labour donated by the men of the congregation, using wood felled and sawn locally. St. James Anglican Church was dedicated on August 31, 1883.

4D · BAPTIST CHURCH

The boom of 1874 brought Henry Graham and his family to Kinmount. They spearheaded the drive to organize a Baptist congregation. In 1877, Rev. George Burns became the town's first Baptist preacher. Services were held in the Presbyterian church until they opened their own house of worship in 1888. This building still stands at the corner of the Monck Road (Highway 503) and Crego Street. In 1919, it was sold for $650 to the Masonic Order, who still own and use it.

The congregation reorganized in 1936 and built the second Baptist church just around the corner from the Anglican church. In 1993, the Baptists sold their church and moved into a schoolhouse (closed earlier that year) at the top of the hill on Highway 503 west of Highway 121.

4E · RAILWAY STATION

The station opened when the Victoria Railway reached Kinmount in 1876. Typical in size and design of many small-town railway stations of the period, it was the only significant survivor of Kinmount's four devastating fires. When a small wooden bridge between Kinmount and Howland Junction was washed out in 1978, the railway line was shut down and the station was closed. The municipality bought the station, which is now used by the Kinmount Lions Club and by local seniors' groups. A tourist information centre opened in the station in the summer of 1995.

The Kinmount Station opened when the Victoria Railway arrived from Lindsay in 1876.

At the north end of the station is a blacksmith shop. This is no historical display, but a working smithy where Kevin Robillard makes his living creating tools and decorative pieces. Visitors who want to see this ancient trade being practised are welcome to drop in.

A scale model of the Victoria Railway from Kinmount north was built in 1994 by the Kinmount Model Railroad Club with the financial support of the Kinmount Lions. They hope to find a permanent home for the model at the fairgrounds in Kinmount.

Kinmount's railway station has managed to survive the town's four major fires and the Great Flood of 1928. This train is northbound. In the background between the station and the train can be seen the roofs of Austin's Mill. Photo courtesy Guy Scott.

4F · AUSTIN'S MILL

Austin's Mill stands in glorious decrepitude at the top of the falls just downriver from the railway station. It is the third sawmill to occupy this site. The first was built in 1874 by W.H. Greene, a prominent lumberman from Fenelon Falls. Ownership passed through several hands until 1893, when it was purchased by William Craig and John Austin for $1,500.

The mill was destroyed by fire in 1908 and rebuilt. A year later, Austin bought Craig out for $4,000. In its heyday, the Austin Mill needed 12,000 logs to keep its saws humming for a season—April to November. Logs were stored in the Burnt River, sometimes backed up all the way to Three Brothers Falls, several miles upriver. The dressed lumber was shipped out on the railway.

A mill operated on this site from 1874 to the mid-1970s. The first two were destroyed by fire; the third, decaying for two decades, is the focus of a local effort to create a historic park.

Austin's Mill stands on the left in this picture on an old postcard. There are so many logs in the river that it looks as though one could walk across to the other bank. The sawn lumber was loaded into railway cars on the siding at right. Photo courtesy Guy Scott.

Between the mill itself and its shanties (camps where the men who felled the trees in winter lived), the Austin Mill quickly became the town's largest employer. It spawned a group of tenement blocks on the hill to the west called the Terrace, where many of the mill workers and their families rented apartments.

During the Depression in the 1930s, the mill closed for two years, throwing many people out of work. Just when it looked as though it might be out of business forever, the government saved the day by contracting with Austin for the lumber to build the camps to house the workers for its local road schemes.

The second mill lasted until it went up in flames in the Great Fire of 1942, which started in one of the mill's sawdust piles. The Austins rebuilt once more and operated until the mid-1970s. In 1994, the entire community undertook a commitment to develop a historic park including both the mill and the railway station.

4G · KINMOUNT HOUSE

This site was one of the first settled in Kinmount and the location of the first business in the community. John Hunter, whom local historian Guy Scott calls the

Handsome Kinmount House hints at the grandeur the village knew before the devastating fires of 1917 and 1942. The house has been restored to its Edwardian elegance over the past decade.

founder of Kinmount, came in the late 1850s. He owned the first mill and built an inn-cum-tavern-cum-store where the house is.

In 1872, Hunter sold all his holdings to William Cluxton and moved to Los Angeles. When the railroad arrived in the village in 1876, Cluxton had his property laid out into building lots and did very nicely. He also gave his name to the street that runs past the front door.

The front two-thirds of the present house were built around the turn of the century by Michael Mansfield, who, with his brother, had a hotel and general store on the main street. The next owner, innkeeper and publican Fred Dettman, added on the back third. He owned the house until 1942, when it was bought by Harry and Ethel Butts, who had lost their hotel in the last of Kinmount's fires. In addition to providing a home for their family of three girls and a boy, they ran it as a boarding house, including among their clientele the schoolteachers of the day.

After Ethel passed away, Harry stayed for another 12 years, then moved to a nursing home. In 1985, Patrick Healey purchased the house and restored it to its earlier beauty. As a bed-and-breakfast, Kinmount House continues to be a gathering place for visitors to the area.

4 H · St. Patrick's Roman Catholic Church

The first Roman Catholic parish in the area was formed in 1879 at Galway, 5 miles south and east of Kinmount. Irish settlers had already been living and worshipping there for about three decades. In 1883, a church was built and, in 1901, at the instigation of Father O'Leary, the parish headquarters was moved from Fenelon Falls to Galway.

O'Leary was an excellent woodsman and a crack shot—one of those "muscular Christians" of the late 19th and early 20th centuries.

Eight years later, however, a new priest decided he would rather live in Kinmount. St. Patrick's Roman Catholic Church was built in 1910 and the rectory next door two years later. On the evening of Easter Day in 1930, only a year after it had been renovated, the church at Galway burned down, and the sad decision was taken not to rebuild. Since then, the parish has had its headquarters in Kinmount.

4 I · Cemeteries

The Catholic cemetery, across the highway from St. Patrick's, was opened in 1934, superceding the one at Galway.

Highway 121 divides Kinmount's Protestant cemetery. The "old" one, to the east, was established in 1862 on an acre of ground purchased from John Hunter. Unlike many pioneer cemeteries, it is complete: the first settler who died is buried in Plot 1, the second in Plot 2, and so on. No settlers were buried in improvised plots on family farms. By about 1920, the first cemetery was full and so the "new" one was opened across the road.

4 J · Kinmount United Church

Built in 1876, Kinmount United Church is one of the oldest surviving structures in the village. As the only local house of worship at the time, it was shared by all denominations. Before it was built, the Presbyterians had been holding services at various sites since as far back as 1859.

For their part, the Methodists had organized in 1870. They used the Presbyterian church until 1886, then moved to the Baptist church. Their numbers were never very large and, in 1903, they had to sell their parsonage. By 1910, the Methodist congregation had dissolved; the remaining adherents joined the Presbyterian congregation.

4K · KINMOUNT FAIRGROUNDS

The Kinmount Fair is the chief pride of the community. It was first held on October 14, 1879, in the field that eventually became the "new" cemetery. By 1900, the Kinmount Fair had outgrown these quarters and the present fairgrounds were purchased under the leadership of Fred Dettman. After the lot was logged and stumped, the first priority was to build a race-track!

Fairs all over the province suffered during the Depression and many were discontinued. Despite the tough times, the Kinmount Fair not only survived, but managed to make improvements to the grounds. It wasn't always easy: one year the secretary had to accept a quilt in lieu of her annual salary.

In the 1950s, an aggressive new group of fair directors began to expand the event into an amalgam of urban and rural values. Chief among their efforts were new buildings and top-notch entertainment. In 1972, to mark the 100th anniversary of the Somerville Agricultural Society, the CBC televised the popular Tommy Hunter Show from here. The Kinmount Fair, now held on the Labour Day weekend, continued to grow and has been for several years the 20th-largest agricultural fair in Ontario.

5 · MONCK ROAD

The Monck Road, now Highway 503, was one of the 13 colonization roads built in the mid-1800s by the government of

The size of the track at the Kinmount Fairgrounds when this picture was taken in 1905 shows the prominence of horse-racing on the fair's calendar in the early days. The large tent at the left housed the merry-go-round. The dirt road in front of the fence is the Monck Road, now Highway 503. Some of the stumps in the foreground are still in the woods along the highway, preserved as charcoal after one of Kinmount's fires. Photo courtesy Keith Stata.

The Monck Road in the 1880s. This group is so well dressed, one might assume they were out for a Sunday drive in the country. Photo courtesy Guy Scott.

Upper Canada to pave the way for settlement. It was intended to go from Lake Couchiching to the Mississippi Road, east of Bancroft. But, like the Peterson Road farther north, it was never properly maintained and quickly fell into disuse. Small sections of it still bear the name in Norland, Kinmount, Gooderham, and Bancroft.

6 · FURNACE FALLS

This beautiful roadside spot on the Irondale River was once part of the Carr homestead. Even then, it was a favourite place among locals and tourists for picnics. But the Carrs didn't mind as long as people didn't leave a mess.

One day, Harold Carr, who had inherited the homestead from his parents, saw a family there and went over to say hello. He recognized the patriarch of the family as Leslie Frost, MPP for Victoria–Haliburton and premier of the province of Ontario. Harold and the premier talked about what a lovely spot this would be for a park and even went so far as to talk price. Before leaving, the premier assured Harold that he would take care of it.

Back at Queen's Park, Frost put the appropriate minister onto the case. But politics being politics, pretty soon the whole thing was mired in bureaucracy. By the time someone got back to Harold, the price wasn't anything like what he and the premier had agreed on. So Harold said no.

Eventually the paths of Harold Carr and Premier Frost crossed again. Naturally, the premier asked how things were going with the park, so Harold told him what had happened. When he got back to the office, the premier made a phone call or two. In no time, Harold had his original deal, and the province became the owner of this pretty spot for us all to enjoy.

7 · IRONDALE

Charles Pusey was a Pennsylvanian who set about to expand his father-in-law's iron ore company. In 1881, he formed the Toronto Iron Company with other American investors to follow up on reports of iron deposits in Snowdon Township. Aided by Henry S. Howland, who later married one of his daughters, Pusey located an iron ore body near Devil's Creek and established a mine.

In addition to the mine site, Pusey bought Lots 29 and 30 in Concession V for a townsite and had them surveyed and divided into lots. Not at all enamoured of the area's original name and hoping for a future metropolis, he rechristened the community—and the river—Irondale.

The town did indeed grow. At its height, it included homes, stores, hotels, mills, the church, the railway station, and other town buildings. Then the mines failed, and although the I.B.&O. Railway, which Pusey and Howland had built, brought some prosperity to the area, eventually most people left Irondale to seek their fortunes elsewhere.

7A · ST. JOHN'S ANGLICAN CHURCH

The only building still standing from the thriving community Charles Pusey created is St. John's Anglican Church. The handsome white building looks rather odd now, standing alone up against the foot of the ridge.

When Pusey's wife, Ruth, arrived at Irondale in the mid-1880s, she declared that a church should be built. It opened in 1887, the product of her initiative and generosity. Her obituary in the Peterborough Examiner in 1892 reported the central role she had played: "She was a member of the English church and showed her fidelity by procuring through her own efforts, and largely by her own means, the erection of a new church at Irondale. . . . She was a most amiable character, large-hearted, kind and unselfish, almost to a fault."

Though Ruth Pusey's leanings were towards the Anglican side, the church has always been for all denominations.

Sometime between 1924 and 1935, according to photographic evidence, the building got its first coat of white paint. The belfry was a still-later addition and the church hall at the southeast corner was put on in the mid-1970s. Other than that, little has been done to change the structure over the years.

8 · MILBURN ROAD

This route to Gelert and Minden takes you through 6 miles of uninhabited back country. It is a well-maintained gravel

St. John's Anglican Church, built in 1887, is all that remains of the bustling town of Irondale, created by Charles Pusey in the 1880s to serve the people who worked in his nearby iron mines.

road, but closed in winter and muddy in spring.

9 · GELERT

Gelert's heyday began and ended with the Victoria Railway. (The "g" is hard and the accent is on the first syllable—GEL-ert. At least that's how the old-timers pronounce it.) The town owed its importance to two factors: it was the only stop between Kinmount and Haliburton with a station agent and it was the stop closest to Minden.

Along Station Street sprouted houses, stores, a blacksmith shop, and a hotel. Two churches were built on the county road, along with the school, the Orange Lodge, and other general stores. A stage coach ran the 7 miles from Minden to Gelert, ferrying passengers in both directions. The village was also a centre for shipping out lumber and cattle. There was a mill on the Drag River just north of the railway bridge; at its busiest, the whole area from the mill to the station—a good quarter-mile in length and almost as broad—would be piled high with stacks of lumber.

Before the Second World War, service on the Victoria Railway had already been reduced to one train a day; after the war, it became sporadic, as roads improved and cars, buses, and trucks began to supplant the railroad. The last passenger train went through Gelert in the early 1960s and the last freight train in the late 1970s.

The train station was dismantled and sold for materials. Schrader's store was badly burned and closed. In 1968, Gelert United Church was closed and moved up to the Valley Road, where it served as a community centre until it burned down a few years later. St. John's Anglican Church was closed and sold by the Synod in Toronto into private hands.

The two schools on the county road are now owned by the municipality. The older frame one, built in 1890, is used as a storage shed; the newer stone one, built in 1950, housed the municipal office until 1995 and is now the community hall.

Gelert was the only town with a station agent between Kinmount and Haliburton. Nothing remains today of the handsome station, shown here on a sunny day in the 1930s. This view looks south towards Kinmount. Photo courtesy John Francis.

CHAPTER THREE

CIRCLE TOUR FROM MINDEN: MOORE FALLS, NORLAND, BULLER, MINERS BAY

Distance: 63 kilometres (38 miles)

Old highways have a particular appeal for me. This tour picks out some remnants of the old routes and combines well-travelled highways with little-known byways.

Deep Bay Road follows the shore of Gull Lake's Deep Bay as it winds its way north through cottage country and farmland to Minden.
Photo courtesy Carol Moffatt.

According to the earliest road maps, Deep Bay Road was the way to get from Minden to Moore Falls in the days when roads were rutted, unsurfaced, and ungraded, and the motorist had to be his own pathfinder and mechanic. The route of Highway 35 from Moore Falls to Norland has been changed a few times over the past 60 years. On the way back, after a trip into the past of a vanished hamlet, the tour takes a short detour along an old shoreline route.

1 · RACKETY CREEK

Rackety Trail offers a brief detour from the main trip. About 1 1/2 miles along the road, there is a pretty falls as the waters of Little Bob Lake tumble down Rackety Creek from the dam to Gull Lake. There is a small picnic area beside the dam.

2 · LITTLE BOB LAKE SCHOOL

The private home opposite the end of Bob Lake Road was one of seven schools in Lutterworth Township. This one was known as the Little Bob Lake School.

3 · MOORE LAKE INN

This handsome inn was built in 1950 by Frances Adamson. Her parents, William and Hilda McDiarmid, had bought the property in 1941 from the estate of Nellie Jones, granddaughter of John Leary, who received the original land grant in 1873. The Leary family had run a tavern here decades earlier.

There was a house on the property when the McDiarmids first bought it. Part of it was kept and added to for the hotel. Adamson called her resort hotel Beverly Park Lodge at the suggestion of her grandmother, who lived in Boston and spent her summers by the ocean at Beverly, Massachusetts.

Beverly Park Lodge was open each summer from Victoria Day to just after Thanksgiving. Its regular guests included the parents of children at Kilcoo Camp. Frances and her husband, Ken, operated the lodge into the mid-1980s. After ten years as Moore Lake Inn, the building has recently been renovated and reopened as Oldham's Inn.

THE AMERICAN COLONY, MOORE LAKE

Among the first "tourists" in the Haliburton Highlands were a group of Americans from Pennsylvania who came to Moore Lake for a month every summer, starting in the 1890s. The story

The ties the men are wearing suggest that this al fresco meal enjoyed in 1898 by the Clarks and the Shorts took place on a Sunday. The Sabbath was strictly observed by the members of the American Colony, who came to camp and cottage on Moore Lake starting in the late 1890s. Photo courtesy Hugh Wilmot.

begins with the Reading family from Toronto, who camped on Owen Wessell's farm during the summers from 1890 to 1893. The Readings brought friends named Wallis, who built the first cottage on the lake, and it was through Windlow Russell, a brother-in-law of the Wallises, that the Americans first came. Russell had moved from Toronto to Kane, Pennsylvania. When he came back for the summer, he brought with him Dr. Thomas Kane, who in subsequent years brought anywhere from 25 to 40 of his relatives and friends to spend a month here each summer. One of these friends, A.D. Clark, and Windlow Russell bought 50 acres on Moore Lake for $1 an acre from Owen Wessell. Over the next 25 years, the two partners sold off lakefront

Several of the members of the American Colony at Moore Lake dispose of chicken sandwiches and other victuals during a picnic at Rackety Creek. Thomas Kane is the second person to the right of the tree. Windlow Russell sits beside him drinking from his cup. Photo courtesy Hugh Wilmot.

lots to others in the group, who built cottages along the shore. Thomas Kane's original straightforward frame cottage still stands on the west shore, as does A.D. Clark's handsome two-storey stone house, built to reflect his considerable wealth. It had a gravity-fed pressurized system that provided running water, several outbuildings (including maids' quarters), and a stone gazebo high on a cliff overlooking the lake—a favourite spot for morning coffee, carried up the hill by the maids.

The Beverly Park Hotel, owned by Frances Adamson, was built for her by Burt Schroter in 1950. The Leary family had the original homestead and ran a tavern here decades earlier. Photo courtesy Frances Adamson.

4 · ELLIOT FALLS

Elliot Falls is the site of a Trent–Severn Waterway dam, a small hydro station, and a park. The first generating station here was completed in 1904 to supply power to the Raven Lake Portland Cement Company. (This Raven Lake is the one 13 miles south in Victoria County, not the one several miles to the north above the Frost Centre.) The company ceased operations in 1914, but the generating station continued to operate and provided power to 500 homes in the surrounding area until 1928.

In 1931, the station was sold to Ontario Hydro. But it was never economically viable, and so, in the 1960s, the site was

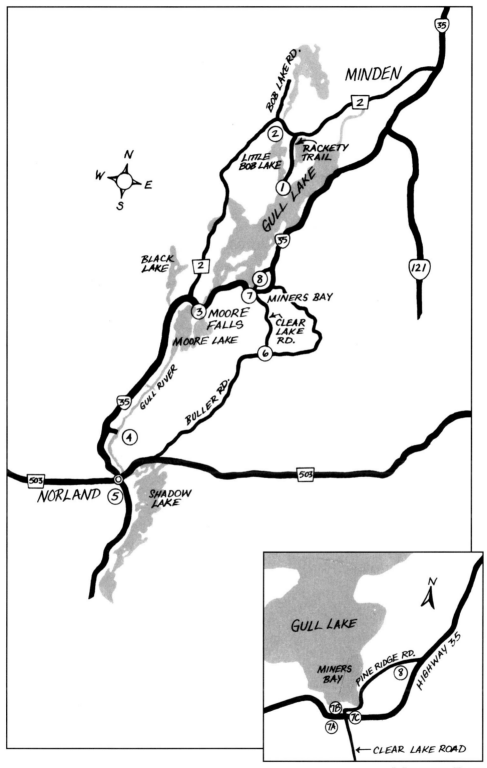

·MINERS BAY·

Elliot Falls is a scenic spot that offers visitors a park, a boat launch, the skeleton of an old power station, and an operating power station.

taken over by the Ministry of Natural Resources, who still look after the park. In 1988, the station was released to private interests—namely, the Elliott Falls Power Commission—for redevelopment.

5 · NORLAND

Though there was a sprinkling of settlers in the area beforehand, the founding of Norland can be traced to the arrival in 1857 of Alexander A. McLauchlin. He was a man of substance from the village of Oakwood, just west of Lindsay. Seeing potential in the waterfalls here, he had a sawmill built at the west end of the present bridge. McLauchlin was also Norland's first postmaster, a member of the first council, builder of the town's first house and grist mill (in addition to the sawmill), and the man who gave the town its name. He even tried to get the railway extended from Coboconk, but in that endeavour he failed.

The settlers in this area came from a mixture of English and Irish back-grounds; surprisingly, two-thirds of them had been born on this side of the ocean, the second generation of immigrant families. The first census, in 1861, reported 407 people. Population peaked at 957 in 1881 and has never returned to that level.

5A · PIONEER BAPTIST CHURCH

The first conversion to the Baptist faith in Norland took place in 1887, the result of missionaries coming west from Kinmount. Until they built their first church over half a century later, the congregation met in the Orange Hall, the Salvation Army barracks, or the Women's Institute Hall.

In 1938, Fred, one of the four Le Craw brothers, donated land on the north side of town for a church and a parsonage. The log parsonage was ready in September 1939 and the church opened in December 1941. In spite of the constant penury of the church coffers, a debt of only $25 was outstanding. It would be another three years before the building was truly completed.

In 1956, an addition was built at the back of the church to increase the space for the Sunday school. In 1990, the large grey addition to the south was built to house the main sanctuary and the original log church became a church hall. Though still owned by the church, the parsonage is now rented as a residence.

5B · NORLAND UNITED CHURCH

In the fall of 1862, a log church called Mount Pleasant Chapel was built south of Norland by the New Connexion Methodists. In 1870, the chapel was closed for unspecified reasons and, two years later, another log church was built at the site of the present church.

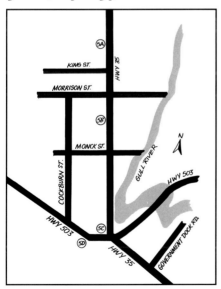

· NORLAND

But the New Connexion Methodists were about to disappear in the face of harsh economic reality. In *The Land Between*, a history of the surrounding townships, F.V. Le Craw puts succinctly the problem faced a century ago by rural churches everywhere.

By the mid-1880s, when the local population was at its peak and roads were improved, the lot of the minister had improved immensely and the Churches generally were in a healthy state. However, hard times were soon to appear, caused by wholesale migrations to the west and dwindling prosperity of those who remained. The result was unions, mutual co-operation, and closures. There were simply too many Churches with too few adherents.

Norland was home to three species of Methodist—New Connexion, Wesleyan,

and Episcopal. By 1875, the first two had combined forces and, nine years later, the third had joined the fold. During the summer and fall of 1885, the combined congregation erected the present Norland United Church directly behind the log church of 1872, which was then torn down.

5C · NORLAND TRADING COMPANY

There has been a store on this site continuously since 1903. Before that, a hotel and tavern called the Adair House stood here from 1864 to 1884, when it burned down. James Ross then built a store, which lasted three years before it too burned. In 1903, George Allely built this two-storey brick building and opened a store. At the rear, there was a long

Ted Le Craw poses for his son Vernon's camera in the mid-1930s behind the counter of the store he and his brother Jim had bought from George Allely in 1914. The store remained in the family for nearly 70 years. It is now the Norland Trading Company. Photo courtesy F.V. Le Craw.

drive-shed with a stable and an oil shed.

In 1914, Allely sold to the Le Craw brothers, Jim and Ted, and moved to Lindsay. The store remained in the Le Craw family for nearly 70 years. In 1939, the brothers dissolved their partnership, leaving Ted with the store until his death in 1943. His wife ran the business until their son Vernon returned from the war and took over in 1946. In 1982, he sold it to Lorne and Rena Parno, who gave the store its present name.

5D · S.S. No. 1
LAXTON–NORLAND

This stone school was built in 1908 to replace the frame one that had been built in 1874 on the hill slightly to the east. Fifteen cords of "good stone" were bought from John Perkins at $4 a cord and the school was put up by Dick Teague, a local stonemason, assisted by Jack Goddard. Robert Morrow was paid $897 for all the carpentry work.

The one-room school served well enough until the late 1950s, when the effects of the postwar population boom hit. In 1960, a room was added to accommodate the lower grades. The basement was converted to an entrance hall and a furnace room and boys' and girls' washrooms were installed. Five years later, S.S. No. 1 became the Area Consolidated School and two more classrooms were added. Each of the four rooms served two grades. In 1992, the Norland school was finally closed; students are now bused to the new Ridgewood School in Coboconk and the stone building has become the municipal office.

EVENTS

The annual *Horse Pull*, held the second Saturday in July, shows off the power and stamina of light and heavy horses from around the province.

For a hundred years, Buller was the centre of a flourishing farming community. At one time, it had its own school and post office.

6 · BULLER

This quiet crossroads was the centre of a flourishing farming settlement from the 1860s into this century, with over a dozen families settled on the surrounding farms. Though Buller never had a church or a store, it did have a school and, from 1900 to 1929, its own post office. The school, which closed around 1960, when Lutterworth Central School was built, still stands at the intersection of Buller Road and Clear Lake Road and is now a private home.

7·MINERS BAY

There weren't many settlers in this area until after the railway reached Coboconk in 1872, when the government finally saw fit to continue the Cameron Road from the county line to Minden. Though David and Jane Galloway officially received a Crown grant in 1881, it is probable that they came here from Norland well before that, perhaps as early as 1873. The Galloways started a store where Miners Bay Lodge is now. He became the community's first postmaster in 1908. The district also boasted a school and a Catholic church.

7A·MINERS BAY LODGE

In 1911, the Galloways sold their fledgling business to the Hopkins brothers and James Mark of Kinmount. Soon after the end of the First World War, the trio was accommodating summer guests. In 1928, Mary Tracy, a relative of the Galloways, and her husband, Herb, acquired the property and named it Bay View Hotel.

In 1937, John E. Windsor, a Methodist minister from Ohio who had come to Miners Bay every year since 1926 (and would keep coming every year until 1971), told his friends William Henry and Erna Cornelia Wunker of Cincinnati that this lodge might be available. In 1938, the Tracys sold to the Wunkers. William and Erna renamed the resort Miners Bay Lodge for the arm of Gull Lake at its doorstep. Nearly 60 years later, the Wunker family still own and operate the resort, one of the oldest in the county.

7B·MINERS BAY CHURCH

This tiny stone church was built in 1906 by stonemasons Joseph Valentine and Duncan Prentice. The date is inscribed in the glass of a window high on the side of the building. The land was provided by the Galloways, and materials, money, and additional labour were donated by the congregation. In its early years, the church was part of the Baptist mission based in Kinmount; the first minister to come here, and the man who may have spearheaded the building of the church, was Rev. Thomas France.

In 1928, the church trustees sold the property to the Home Mission Board, who still own it. However, when the Wunkers arrived to take over the lodge in 1938, the church was unused and in disrepair. They made an arrangement to take care of the building in return for permission to hold services there for their guests. This arrangement, renewed every year, is still in effect. The Wunker family has also done a great deal of work to restore and refurbish the building. Nowadays, during the summer season, services are held every Sunday evening and the church is used two nights a week for Bible study.

7C·MINERS BAY ROCK CUT

This spectacular rock cut was created when the new route of the highway was blasted through in 1970. Michael Easton of the Ontario Geological Survey describes it as a miniature version of what can be found geologically throughout the whole area.

It's like a cake full of fruit and nuts. The rocks are both cooked up and broken up. There are all these dark grey chunks—the granite and sedimentary rocks—in a white matrix of calcite marble or cooked-up limestone. A cut like this helps us understand what we find in the bush when we see different kinds of rocks in the same area.

The dramatic rock cut on Highway 35 frames Miners Bay Lodge, which has been owned and operated by the Wunker family since 1938 and is one of the oldest resorts in the county.

Instead of turning right (north) on Highway 35, go straight across onto the original route of the highway. The old route follows the shore of Miners Bay on Gull Lake past the former Pine Ridge Resort and Hounsell's School (see No. 8 below), and comes back to Highway 35, which leads north to Minden.

8 · HOUNSELL'S SCHOOL

Another of the seven Lutterworth schools still stands beside the old highway. It was named for the Hounsell family, who farmed this land from 1904. The school is now a private home.

CHAPTER FOUR

CIRCLE TOUR FROM MINDEN: HORSESHOE, TWELVE MILE, BLAIRHAMPTON, BETHEL

Distance: 35 kilometres (21 miles)

From Minden, this tour follows some of the original roads that lead north from the village and comes back through the rural district of Blairhampton.

1· ORILLIA WATER, LIGHT, AND POWER DAM

The Orillia Water, Light, and Power dam, hidden in the valley to the south of Horseshoe Lake Road, was built in 1934 and 1935 to harness the power of the falls at this site for electricity. For over seven decades before that, the 68-foot fall of water had been used to power a succession of mills.

According to Jane Fairfield's report in the *Tweedsmuir History of Minden*, the first sawmill was built on the south side of the river in 1860. The following year, a four-storey grist mill was built on the north side. The two were joined by the

Allsaw Road bridge, which spanned the rapids. It was over this bridge that the road leading north from Minden originally ran.

For nearly 70 years, settlers throughout the area and as far away as Wilberforce and Gooderham brought their logs here to be sawn into lumber and their grain to be ground into flour. In 1867, both mills were sold to Hugh Workman and the site became known as Workman's Falls. From 1893 until the late 1920s, the mills were owned by the Stinson family. By then, both agriculture and logging were in decline. In 1929, the mills were demolished and the machinery sold. The millstones that had produced Sunrise Flour ended up as fill in a parking lot.

To make way for the dam, the bridge across the river was demolished and this road was constructed on the north side

Shortly after it was built in the mid-1930s, the Orillia Water, Light, and Power dam was featured on a postcard of that time. Photo courtesy Marie Emmerson.

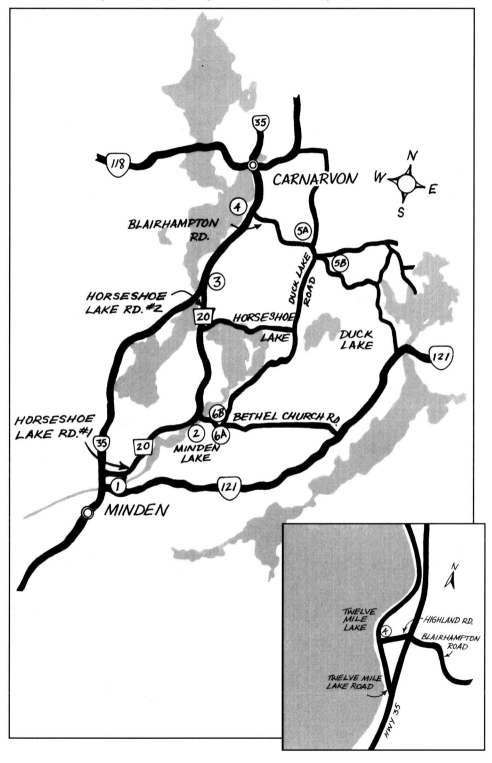

The Orillia Water, Light, and Power dam was built in the art deco style in the mid-1930s at the site of Workman's Falls on the Gull River above Minden to provide electricity to Orillia.

of the river. Men hired to build the dam worked around the clock on ten-hour shifts for top wages of 35 cents an hour. On August 21, 1935, the floodgates were opened and the turbines in the stately art deco building began to turn, producing the power to light up the city of Orillia, 60 miles away, as well as the local community. In the great blackout of 1965, which left most of Southern Ontario and the northeastern United States in darkness, the lights of Orillia continued to shine with the power from Workman's Falls.

2 · MINDEN WILD WATER PRESERVE

These rapids were the site of many a river drive from the 1860s until 1929, when the last load of logs passed this way. They used to be known as Sanderson's Rapids, in memory of a river driver who, it is said, was drowned here around 1912 while doing that dangerous work and was buried on the shore nearby.

The dam at the top of rapids was originally one of dozens of timber-crib dams built by the logging companies to control the flow of water and make it possible to run logs throughout the snow-free seasons, instead of having to rely solely on the annual spring run-off. (The Mossom Boyd Company's dams alone raised water levels 7 feet over 80 square miles of Haliburton County.) In 1905, control of the dams passed to the federal government. The rotting timber cribs were replaced with concrete dams, which are now under the authority of the Trent-Severn Waterway.

In 1980, the site was bought by the Ontario White Water Affiliation, and nature was renovated to create a world-class slalom course for canoes and kayaks—the only such course in Eastern

The Minden Wild Water Preserve is a world-class slalom course for canoes and kayaks, where World Cup events and national and provincial championships are held. For many years around the turn of the century, log drives passed this way during the snow-free seasons. The last one was held in 1929.

Canada. National and provincial championships are held here regularly and it is also a frequent location for World Cup events.

And any weekend—spring, summer, or fall; rain or shine—kayakers and canoeists in brightly coloured gear practise in the tumbling waters. In July 1987, the Duchess of York was one of those practising here. She came on a surreptitious visit to get her first taste of white-water canoeing before she and Prince Andrew went on a canoe trip on the Thelon River in the Northwest Territories.

Horseshoe Lake Road passes over a narrows between Mountain Lake and Horseshoe Lake. The present one-lane steel bridge was preceded by this log bridge. The photograph, taken around 1920, looks towards Horseshoe Lake. Photo courtesy Ted Heaven.

3 · HIGHWAY 35

Before 1931, when work began on Highway 35, there was no continuous road north of Minden and the road south of the village was more suited to horse-drawn wagons than to cars. In 1912, the *Official Automobile Guide of Canada* issued this warning to prospective motorists: "From Coboconk to Norland, a distance of five miles, the road is gravelled; beyond that there is nothing but sand." In fact, the sand ended not too far past Norland, to be replaced by deep ruts, jutting rocks, steep hills, and rough corduroy. Like virtually all the roads in Haliburton at the time, this one was only one lane wide, with shoulders barely wide enough for passing when two cars met.

Building Highway 35 served two purposes. First, it was one of several Depression-era make-work projects across Ontario funded under the Colonization Roads Act. Second, the route was deliberately laid out to follow the lakes in order to stimulate tourism.

Thirteen military-style work camps were built at intervals between the county line and Dorset to house the labourers; the headquarters were in Minden. Each camp consisted of bunkhouses, an office, a stable, a blacksmith shop, separate living quarters for the "key men" (superintendent and foremen), a cookhouse and mess hall, and the cook's quarters.

In the beginning, labourers were paid $10 a month plus room and board (though a man with a team of horses might get double that), but this was soon reduced to $5. Purchases at the camp commissary were deducted from their wages. The only real perk the men enjoyed was a good, substantial meal three times a day from the hands of the camp cook. All in all, conditions were not unlike those in the logging camps of the previous generation.

And the word *labourer* is apt: these men worked by hand, with picks, shovels, wheelbarrows, and drills driven by sledgehammers. Only horses for hauling and dynamite for blasting provided relief from physical toil.

Construction continued until 1934, when a change of government at Queen's Park shut down the camps. But the road was substantially complete. The impact was immediate. In 1936, A.L. McDougall, the Colonization Road Engineer, wrote, "The most important and outstanding work in the division was the completion of the scenic highway from Coboconk to Dorset. . . . Traffic has increased to such an extent that, on one day early in August, over one thousand motors passed through the village of Minden."

4 · TWELVE MILE CHURCH

Twelve Mile Church began as a Presbyterian church. The land came via a Crown grant made on March 25, 1880, but construction did not begin until September 1890. The original documents chronicling the project reflect a concern for expense proper to the spiritual descendants of John Knox; year in and year out, every penny is accounted for.

Funds were raised through pledges from the men of the congregation, who promised to pay "the sum set beside our name or equivalent in value . . . as soon as the Church is finished or before." The names of 28 men are then listed and, beside them, amounts totalling $116.42. John Johnson was named overseer of the building "at the sum of One Dollar per Day." The building was completed by the end of December 1890, as projected.

The cemetery was laid out in 1901 (although several tombstones predate this, going as far back as 1877), and given the formal name Twelve Mile Lake View Cemetery. Each family plot of eight graves was to cost $1.50, but in 1902 the graveyard was made free to members of the congregation and "strangers" were charged $1.50.

In 1921, four years before the formal union of the Presbyterians, Methodists, and Congregationalists into the United Church of Canada, the little white church was closed and its members joined forces with Zion Methodist in Carnarvon. For many years, it was opened only for funerals.

These days, Twelve Mile Church is used on Sunday evenings in July and August for an informal song service. It's also the site of a wedding or two every summer. It's hard to imagine a more idyllic spot than this for nuptials or for praise, especially as the evening wanes and the setting sun reaches across the water and under the trees.

Opposite the church is one of the most popular public beaches in the area. If the time of day and the weather are right, this makes a great place to stop for a swim and a picnic.

5 · BLAIRHAMPTON

The rural district known as Blairhampton takes its name from the first family to settle in the area. William and Maria (pronounced Ma-rye-ah) Blair, whose descendants still live in the area six generations later, came from Britain and arrived in Port Hope on June 6, 1861. They travelled to Rice Lake by ox-drawn wagon, and their first child, also named William, was born there that year.

By the time their second child, Margaret Ann, arrived in 1863, the Blairs had moved north to homestead in the logged-over wilderness northeast of Minden, on a land grant half a mile south of the intersection that has become known as Church Corner (see No. 5B below). Another four children were later added to the brood. Two more generations of Blairs would be born on this homestead before the family moved to another farm on the north side of nearby Duck Lake.

Duck Lake Road is one of the beautiful back roads that run through Blairhampton. The district has earned a considerable reputation locally as a place where people are likely to get lost.

5A · HILLVIEW FARM

The second family to come to the area were Tom and Ella Voicey. The name of their homestead, Hillview Farm, which is still in the family, is proclaimed on the barn.

5B · CHURCH CORNER

Blairhampton has never had anything approaching even a hamlet, let alone a village. But it did have a geographical centre known as Church Corner. Here stood the first church, built on the southwest corner of the intersection in the 1880s. By the 1890s, the Sunday school could boast an average weekly attendance of 30 children. After the church burned down, a second one was built on the other side of the road around 1907; it was closed in the mid-1960s and is now a private home.

Across the road from the second church (and diagonally across from the first) stood the first schoolhouse—until it burned and a second one was built farther east. When the second school closed in 1953, it had an enrolment of over two dozen. The school is now a private home as well.

There was never a store in Blairhampton—settlers went to Minden for what they couldn't grow or raise—but there was always a post office in one farmhouse or another.

The first car made its appearance about 1910 and was a source of great excitement; children ran the length of a hundred-acre lot to get a look at it. Electricity, on the other hand, didn't arrive until the 1950s.

Blairhampton can boast at least one famous son. Wren Blair, former general manager of the Minnesota North Stars of the National Hockey League, is a great-grandson of William and Maria.

Horseshoe Lake is one of the 500-plus lakes that make the Haliburton Highlands such outstanding cottage country. The lake is bounded on the north by the district of Blairhampton and on the south by the district of Bethel.

6 · Bethel

Bethel is the name given to the district around the south end of Horseshoe Lake. Like Blairhampton, it had its church, its school, and its post office. The church and school were eventually independent buildings, but the post office was accommodated in a series of local homes.

6A · Bethel Church

Pioneering families initially held their worship services in someone's home. Sometimes they were conducted by a minister who, as a mission circuit rider, would travel around the district on foot or on horseback, doing as many services on a Sunday as he could. Other times one of the local men would lead the service. But for the devout, the front parlour could never replace a proper church.

It was this spirit that moved the residents of Bethel to build this log church. In the winter of 1890–91, James Nesbitt, William and Blane Robinson, and Sidney Stevens felled the logs for the building. Teams owned by the three Cox brothers hauled the logs to the site. Thirteen-year-old Samuel Nesbitt drove his father's team of oxen to haul some of the logs over to the mill at Lochlin, where they were sawn into lumber. As soon as the crops were planted in the spring of 1891, a building bee was called for a May morning. The men arrived with broadaxes, saws, ropes, and pike poles. A bench was set up for the carpenters, W.J. Archer and Jim Reynolds, to plane the lumber for the doors and window casings. The 2-inch-thick pine for the original door came from Workman's Mill (where the

For the devout pioneer, only a proper chuch would do. The settlers of the Bethel area built their church in one day in May 1891. For the first service, families came by buggy and wagon, by rowboat and canoe, and by shank's mare.

Orillia Water, Light, and Power dam is now; see No. 1 above). The shingles came from Thompson's Mill (near the present Blairhampton Golf Course, up Duck Lake Road.)

At 11:00 A.M., the women arrived and set up for lunch. They built a fire to boil water for tea and made huge sandwiches of homemade bread and home-cured ham. Cakes and pies—apple and rhubarb and raisin—followed. By evening, their church was complete. Everyone was especially proud of the arched windows, which made them feel that this would be a real church. There was also a drive shed, now long since gone, that could accommodate four teams of horses and also housed the woodshed and the privy.

For the first service, people came by buggy and wagon, by rowboat and canoe. Many families walked, carrying their little ones. A Rev. Mr. Peake led the worship, in which all denominations joined.

Over the decades, improvements were made to the church. The tin roofing, brick chimney, and front porch, for instance, are all later additions.

Shortly after the end of First World War, services gradually stopped and weren't revived until the late 1930s, when an evangelical couple named Gillings received permission to use the church for their services. Use fell off again around 1950, and the church saw its last wedding a few years later, when Victor Peel and Alma Harrison were married.

At times during the four decades since, vandalism has plagued the vacant church. After one particularly wanton attack, it was boarded up. However, the cemetery surrounding the church remains a place of repose and tranquility. Recent grave-markers stand beside headstones dating back to the 1890s, hinting at poignant stories and family tragedies. Perhaps the first grave dug was for Arthur, son of Jonathan and Jane Cox, who died on October 21, 1891, at the age of ten months and eleven days.

6B · BETHEL SCHOOL

As the date on the front of the one-room school across the road from the church indicates, Bethel School was built in 1905. It served the community until the 1950s, when the rural schools were consolidated and school buses were introduced. The school is now a private home.

....

There are those who maintain that Blairhampton is the Bermuda Triangle of Haliburton County. Indeed, people do seem to get lost easily here.

Blairhampton has also had a reputation for terrible roads, and it was certainly well deserved back in the days of corduroy roads—roads made of logs laid across the direction of travel. In the spring, the logs would be swallowed by the mud, and sections of roads would disappear under the rising tide of roadside swamps. That still happens some years in low-lying spots, although the corduroy construction has been gone for some time.

Carrie Munson Hoople, quoted in *The Story of Canadian Roads* by Edwin C. Guillet, described a journey over a corduroy road in this parody of Tennyson's "The Charge of the Light Brigade."

Half a log, half a log, half a log onward / Shaken and out of breath, rode we and wondered. / Ours not to reason why, ours but to clutch and cry / While onward we thundered.

CHAPTER FIVE

HALIBURTON VILLAGE

Thomas Chandler Haliburton was a Nova Scotia Chief Justice who moved to England when he retired. He chaired the company that bought the nine townships of Dysart et alii *and opened up these back woods for settlement. Photo courtesy John Daniel Logan,* Thomas Chandler Haliburton, *Ryerson, 1923.*

The county and the village of Haliburton take their name from Thomas Chandler Haliburton, the Nova Scotia Chief Justice who gained international fame for his humorous stories about Sam Slick, a crafty Yankee trader. In 1842, Haliburton retired to England, where he was elected to the British House of Commons. In 1859, he and a group of fellow investors answered an advertisement placed by Philip Vankoughnet, Upper Canada's Commissioner of Crown Lands. It offered the nine townships of Dysart, Dudley, Harcourt, Guilford, Harburn, Bruton, Havelock, Eyre, and Clyde for sale at 50 cents an acre.

Haliburton and his colleagues incorporated as the Canadian Land and Emigration Company of London, England, and Haliburton was named the first chairman of the company. They proposed to

The main street of Haliburton in the late 1920s or early 1930s. The tall building halfway down the right side of the street was the Grand Central Hotel. First called Haliburton House and then the Anglo-Saxon Hotel, it was renovated and renamed the Grand Central in 1896. In its later years, the building became a Stedman's store. The landmark burned down in the mid-1980s. Photo courtesy National Archives of Canada and Haliburton Highlands Museum.

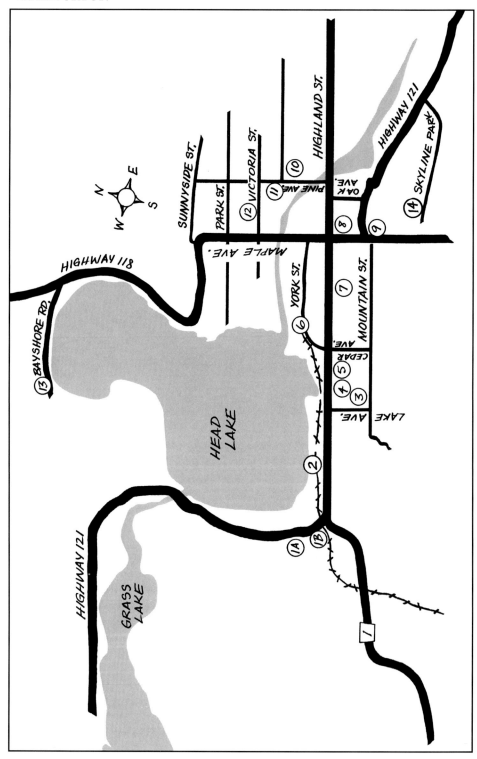

establish model agricultural communities to be settled by English emigrants in these "Back Townships" of Upper Canada.

The fact that none of these financiers, nor any of the people who bought shares in their company, nor any of those contemplating emigration and homesteading in the area had ever set eyes on the territory in question was no deterrent. It seems no one on either side of the Atlantic wanted to take seriously the observation made by surveyor Robert Bell in his report. "The greatest objections that at all exist in respect to the whole territory is the great abundance of rocks."

In 1863, Edward Miles surveyed the town plot into an orderly grid of streets and lots. It looked straightforward enough on paper, but when the first immigrants arrived soon after to take up their land, they found a densely wooded, hilly landscape populated by Algonquians and a few squatters.

Steam Locomotive No. 2616 commemorates the days when the train was a daily feature of life in Haliburton village. The fighter jet was installed here in 1974 as part of the county's centennial celebrations.

1A · STEAM LOCOMOTIVE No. 2616

Built in 1891 by the American Locomotive Company in Dunkirk, New York, Steam Locomotive No. 2616 served on the Canadian National Railway's Belleville-to-Lindsay run. When it was retired in 1960, No. 2616 was purchased by the Haliburton Rotary Club and given a permanent home here to commemorate the opening of the rail link between Lindsay and Haliburton (see No. 2 below).

1B · CF-100 FIGHTER PLANE

This CF-100 jet fighter served as an instructional aircraft with the RCAF's 413 Squadron at Bagotville, Quebec, and North Bay, Ontario, from 1951 to 1961. It was declared surplus and bought for $525 by the Municipality of Dysart *et alii* and Branch 129 of the Royal Canadian Legion. The cost of transporting and installing the plane was ten times the purchase price. It was dedicated on September 1974 as part of the county's centennial celebrations.

2 · VICTORIA RAILWAY

On November 26, 1878, the long-awaited first train of the Victoria Railway steamed from Lindsay into Haliburton village and chugged to a stop in front of the brand-new station. Among the things the railway had brought with it was the very creation of the County of Haliburton itself.

The townships that now form the County of Haliburton had been divided among Peterborough County and Victoria County to the south and the District of Nipissing to the north. Peterborough County had refused to commit its taxpayers to the expense of building a railroad into this sparsely populated region. So the community successfully petitioned the Legislative Assembly in Toronto, and on May 27, 1874, the local electorate voted almost unanimously in favour of becoming a new county. In dividing up the spoils, it was decided that Minden would become the county seat (which it still is) and Haliburton would get the railway.

Alas, the promise of growing prosperity and population heralded by the railway was unfulfilled. People took advantage of the easier transportation to escape the "bust" half of recurring boom-and-bust cycles. Population in Dysart actually declined to a low of 119 in 1881.

A section crew works on the rails outside the Haliburton station in the 1880s. The foreman was George Potts (left). In 1904, Potts hired John Henry Billing to build him a house, which he called Lakeview. Potts was town clerk from 1909 to 1915. Photo courtesy Haliburton Highlands Museum.

The Victoria Railway continued to carry people and goods in and out of the county for exactly a century, but the growing hegemony of the highway and the automobile gradually displaced it. Passenger service was discontinued in 1961, and regular freight service was discontinued in 1972. Freight service was available on demand until 1978, when a small wooden bridge north of Kinmount was washed out. The tracks were torn up in the ensuing decade, and, in 1988, the county purchased the railbed for use as a recreational trail.

3 · ST. GEORGE'S ANGLICAN CHURCH

The beginnings of both the Anglican congregation in Haliburton and their church stem from the Canadian Land and Emigration Company. The company provided the land and a 16-by-24-foot log building, which held up to 90 people. The company paid for Rev. Richard Sandars to come from Toronto and open the new church on New Year's Day 1865.

Forty-two worshippers braved freezing temperatures and snow-clogged roads to attend. The music was provided by the company doctor, an Englishman named John Peake, who led the choir from a unique instrument, an accordion mounted on a frame and operated by a foot-treadle.

The company also agreed to contribute £250 towards the support of any clergyman willing to take up the post and offered the storekeeper's house for a prospective incumbent to live in.

The clergyman sent to Dysart by John Strachan, the Lord Bishop in Toronto, was Frederick Burt, who arrived with his wife, Louisa, in mid-1865. They stayed but a few months at St. George's, moving in November to Minden, where they established the congregation at St. Paul's. It would be another four years before Haliburton again had a resident clergyman.

In March 1869, Rev. Gaden Crawford MacKenzie, his wife, Helen, and their two children found their way to what the Lord Bishop was pleased to call "the remote Township of Dysart." Although he stayed only 18 months, MacKenzie's contribution to the parish was substantial. Under his leadership, the log church was replaced with a frame one designed in the gothic style. Peterborough architect and civil engineer J.E. Belcher drew up the plans free of charge, and Henry Wesley built it for $700. One of Wesley's carpenters was William Roberts, who would be able to claim in a few years that he had worked on all three churches in town. The widow of Thomas Chandler Haliburton came to present a cabinet organ and promised to send a bell.

This building served the congregation for nearly 50 years until it was consumed by fire on January 25, 1920. The Baptists down the hill invited the Anglicans to use their church while they rebuilt. The congregation rallied and rebuilt on the original foundations, but this time their church was of brick. It was opened by the Bishop of Toronto on October 24, 1923.

The parish hall, designed by architect and historian Bruce Napier Simpson, was added in 1967. In 1986, the church was expanded to enlarge the nave. The roof of the sanctuary, much of the furniture, and many of the stained-glass windows date back to the reconstructed building of 1923.

The brick version of St. George's Anglican Church stands on the foundations of the second building, which burned to the ground in 1920.

Next door to the church stands the rectory, built in 1899, probably by William Prust, a skilled carpenter who had emigrated from England in 1873 with his wife, Ellen, and their two children. Many of the original features of the house remain intact in the central brick section between the frame addition put on at the back during the First World War and the large front porch put up in the 1920s.

4 · BAPTIST CHURCH

The Baptist congregation in Haliburton village was established as First Baptist Church on August 18, 1901. They had no church building and held their services in the Orange Hall, McEver's School, Harburn School, or members' homes.

Land on the road at the foot of the hill below St. George's was purchased for a permanent church from Mary Dart. The church was finally built in 1904 and opened the following year, but the outside was not completed until 1909, when Ferdinand Sipe and his committee undertook to face it with brick. Because there was no baptistry in the church itself, baptisms took place in Head Lake, the first one in 1906.

After nearly six decades, it was time to build a new church. The old one had become hard to heat, there was a creek underneath that caused structural problems, and the congregation was growing. On March 12, 1961, Lakeside Baptist Church, which stands on Park Street near the lakefront, was dedicated. Clara Orr was the one person present who had also been part of the first congregation in 1904.

The old building was sold and first became a Western Tire store. It now houses Rachel's Home Bakery. If you look up the laneway beside the bakery, you can still see the original brick under a coat of paint.

5 · LAKEVIEW HOUSE

On the front of the house, above the second-storey windows, the house proclaims its name and its date: *Lakeview 1904.*

George Potts, who would become town clerk from 1909 to 1915, engaged John Billing, the county's master stonemason, to build this house. The exterior of the frame structure was covered with 3 inches of slip-poured concrete and 1 inch of stucco. Billing and his workmen scored the wet stucco to make the building look like stone. Then they put another layer of rough-cast stucco in a slightly darker colour at each corner to simulate quoin corners in stone.

The house was restored in 1983 by cabinetmaker Grant Rae, who, with his wife, Dorothy, a descendant of George Potts, had bought Lakeview that year.

6 · RAILS' END STATION GALLERY

Thanks to the Haliburton Highlands Guild of Fine Arts, the exterior of the old railway station still looks much as it did when it first opened back in 1878. In the mid-1970s, when it became clear that the trains would never run to Haliburton again, members of the fledgling guild took on the project of restoring and renovating the station as a permanent home for their activities.

They raised the necessary funds locally and through Wintario, and, under the direction of Toronto-based architects, had much of the work done by volunteer labour. Every effort was made to be true to the character of the old station, from the colour of the paint to furniture and hardware. Canadian National, owners of the Victoria Railway when it was abandoned, were persuaded to donate objects that related to the railway in its heyday.

Since it opened in July 1979, the Rails' End Station Gallery has been an important cultural centre. It houses two art galleries and a craft shop, as well as providing a home for the continuing activities of the guild and its members.

The old railway station, which now houses the Rails' End Station Gallery, looks much as it did when it first opened in 1878, right down to the colour of the paint.

7 · NIVEN HOUSE

This modest white house, set well back from the street and sandwiched between commercial enterprises of the late 20th century, was built in 1881 for Alexander and Maggie Niven by carpenter James L. Brown at a cost of $300.

Niven had come to Haliburton in 1868 at the age of 32 as resident agent for the Canadian Land and Emigration Company. He also became reeve of the Municipality of Dysart *et alii* and the first warden of the Provisional County of Haliburton.

8 · 45TH PARALLEL

The traffic light at the intersection of Highland Street and Maple Avenue (Highways 121 and 118) is on the 45th parallel. As the sign on top of the gas station at the corner proclaims, it is 3,107 miles to both the North Pole and the Equator.

9 · TOWN HALL

Dysart Town Hall is the second building to serve this purpose on this site. The property was purchased from the land company in the spring of 1869 for $100 and set aside for a town hall, market ground, and public square. The first town hall was a frame structure built in 1871 at a cost of $1,391.93. It was named Lucas Hall, after the community's first reeve and opened on December 6, 1871.

Dysart Town Hall dates to 1897. The single-storey section at the back is a later addition.

This building burned down on July 4, 1895, and was replaced by the current structure. Construction started on May 1, 1897, and the new building was officially opened exactly five months later, on October 1.

10 · HALIBURTON UNITED CHURCH

Like that of all congregations in the United Church of Canada, the story of Haliburton United Church is a tale of two churches: Methodist and Presbyterian.

The Presbyterians were the first to arrive in Haliburton village. They established their congregation in 1868, led by the organizing energies of Alexander Niven. In 1875, they hired carpenter James L. Brown (the same man who would build Niven's house) to erect a church 24 feet by 44 feet.

The early records of the Haliburton Methodist Church were probably destroyed by fire. The first building was erected in 1874 on land across the road from where the arena now stands, which had been given to the congregation six years earlier by the Canadian Land and Emigration Company. This building, 30 feet by 48 feet, burned down in 1909, and, for at least three years, the Methodists rented the Presbyterian church for their services at $1 a week. In 1911 and 1912, they began to build a new church, not on the original site, but here, closer to the Presbyterian building.

On July 10, 1918—seven years before formal church union in June 1925—representatives of both the Presbyterian and Methodist congregations held the first meeting of the Union church. The Presbyterians had held their last service in their old church (where the Masonic Hall now stands) on the last Sunday of June 1918 before joining their new co-adherents in the Methodist building around the corner on Pine Avenue.

In 1948, the front of the church was modified from the original Methodist meeting-hall style by the addition of a chancel, and the interior of the church was redecorated as well. In 1972, the manse next door to the church burned down and the ample Christian Education Building—with Sunday school rooms, a church office, a kitchen and dining hall, and washrooms—was put in its place and connected to the church via a tunnel from one basement to the other. In 1983, the front entranceway to the church was expanded into a narthex and an above-ground passageway to the Christian Education Building constructed.

There had been extensive renovations back in 1967 too. During these renovations, designed and supervised by Bruce Napier Simpson, most of the stained-glass windows were donated. Those honoured in the six windows along the side walls of the church are primarily early pioneers of the congregation. The central window above the altar, however, is for a young member of the congregation, Curtis Way, who died in a car accident that year at the age of 22. At the peak of this window's gothic arch, circumscribed by its own circle of lead, is a picture of the original Presbyterian church of 1875.

11 · OLD IRWIN STORE

In 1880, lumber baron Mossom Boyd and his son-in-law James M. Irwin obtained timber limits and leased the sawmill from the Canadian Land and Emigration Company. To capitalize on the increased economic activity sparked by logging, Irwin built a company store, with a bakery behind, a boarding house next door, and stables on the corner.

Fred Freeman, an English-born bachelor, arrived in the village in 1881 to manage Irwin's general store. He purchased it in 1885 and ran it for the next 52 years. In 1937, Art Gilliam bought the store from Freeman's estate. In 1954, Edward Miller bought it from Gilliam's estate and owned it until 1978, when it was purchased by Don Banks, who operated the store until his death in 1995.

The building, which remains largely in its original state, now houses the Wild Oat Arts Cafe.

Banks' General Store was originally Irwin's store. It was built around 1880 by lumberman James M. Irwin to capitalize on the increased economic activity sparked by logging. In this photograph, Fred Freeman stands in the doorway. Freeman managed the store for Irwin starting in 1881. He bought it in 1885 and retained ownership until 1937.
Photo courtesy Haliburton Highlands Museum.

Banks' General Store has changed little over the past century. Inside, in the midst of present-day wares for sale, is a treasure trove of memorabilia recalling the old days.

12 · ST. ANTHONY'S CATHOLIC CHURCH

The village's Catholic church grew out of the collective labours of the area's Italian community. Between 1908 and 1945, labourers came from Italy to cut hardwood that fed the fires at the Standard Chemical Company's factory in Donald (see Chapter 6, No. 9). Most of the Italians stayed only a season or two, then went home. The half-dozen men who stayed either brought brides from the old country or married local women. The Pasquino and Miscio families came shortly after the turn of the century; the Biagi, Formica, Luna, and Salvatori families arrived after 1918.

The religious needs of these young Catholics were met by priests who visited sporadically from Bancroft and said mass in parishioners' homes. In 1934, Father Lesley J. Kennedy began pushing for a church in Haliburton. He hired a carpenter from Bancroft and asked that all the men donate whatever other labour might be required, setting an example by toting his share of cement.

Nazzareno (Ned) Biagi—called Il Bosso (The Boss) by everyone—donated the land and provided leadership for the project, as he did for much else in the community. The first mass was celebrated on July 16, 1938, even before the frame building was entirely finished.

The cottaging boom that began after the Second World War increased the size of the congregation, at least in the summer, and, in 1957, an addition was constructed at the back of the church that doubled its size. In the late 1970s, it was decided to replace the frame church with the present brick one. This time, the congregation's volunteer efforts focused on fund-raising instead of labour.

Their energy was complemented by the generosity of Haliburton's Protestant congregations. Both the Anglican and United churches gave gifts of money. In addition, St. George's provided the use of their church for services after the old St. Anthony's was torn down in November 1981. The Orange Lodge rented its hall to St. Anthony's for their regular bingo games; then, belying 200 years of anti-Catholic rancour, they donated the collected rent to St. Anthony's building fund, putting a new twist on the idea of forced savings. The new St. Anthony's was formally opened on May 16, 1982.

13 · HALIBURTON HIGHLANDS MUSEUM

The Haliburton Highlands Museum was established in 1967 through the efforts of a core of local history enthusiasts. The Haliburton Rotary Club purchased the Reid House by the lakeshore for the museum's first home. In 1979, the museum moved to its current site near Glebe Park. At the same time, the Reid House was moved here to make way for Rotary Beach.

The main gallery is open all year; it houses interpretive exhibits on the prehistoric eras of the region and collections of artifacts from the county's early days. The Reid House (open spring, summer, and fall) is furnished to represent village life at the turn of the century. The log cabin, log barn, and blacksmith's shop of the Farmstead (open in the summer) were brought from various sites around the county to portray pioneer life.

In addition to the permanent displays, the main gallery preserves a growing collection of historical documents and research papers about the area.

The haunting interior of the log cabin at the Haliburton Highlands Museum portrays early pioneer life in the Haliburton Highlands. The cabin is part of the museum's Farmstead, a collection of original buildings brought together from various parts of the county.

14 · SKYLINE PARK

Skyline Park provides an overview of the town and the distant hills, along with amenities for picnickers, including tables, outhouses, and a barbecue pit.

EVENTS

The **Haliburton Highlands School of Fine Arts** runs for six weeks each summer, from the beginning of July to mid-August. It offers a variety of courses one to two weeks long in a wide range of arts and crafts. The school's reputation and beautiful setting draw people from far and wide.

The **Highland Games** are held each July at Glebe Park. The games feature pipe-and-drum performances, Highland dancing, Celtic music, children's games, and heavy events such as the caber toss.

The **Haliburton Rotary Carnival** is held on the first Wednesday in August at various sites around town. It includes the Rotary Mile (a supper-hour fun run through town) followed by a parade.

The **Bluegrass Festival** is held annually for three days in early August at Glebe Park. Headliners and lesser lights perform in the bandshell, which faces out to the hillside amphitheatre.

Skyline Park looks west and north over Haliburton village and across a panoramic spread of hills. The view is spectacular in autumn.

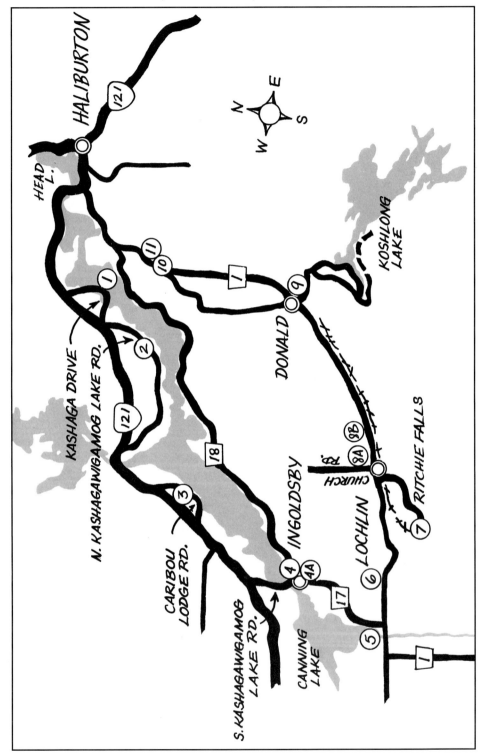

CHAPTER SIX

CIRCLE TOUR FROM HALIBURTON: KASHAGAWIGAMOG, INGOLDSBY, LOCHLIN, DONALD

Distance: 50 kilometres (30 miles)

A trip around Lake Kashagawigamog goes through communities that have surrounded it for over a hundred years. To follow the north shore of the lake more closely, take Kashaga Drive, North Kashagawigamog Road, and Caribou Lodge Road (called Old Allsaw Road at its west end).

1 · LAKE KASHAGAWIGAMOG

Before the Victoria Railway reached Haliburton in 1878, Lake Kashagawigamog provided the first link in the transportation route to Minden. George S. Thompson worked on the boats that carried people and goods in both directions. He described a typical trip in his 1895 book, *Up To Date or The Life of a Lumberman.*

By our early rising we would take advantage of the calm nights to row the freight boat down to the storehouse at the foot of Lake Kashog [Kashagawigamog], sixteen miles, before the wind would rise, so that on our up trip we would have the fair west wind mostly prevalent in these summer months in that section. So we often used to run the round trip of thirty-two miles and be back in Haliburton and unload our cargo before noon. . . . The mail in those days was tri-weekly—Tuesdays, Thursdays and Saturdays. On mail days we usually ran two boats — a freight boat and a skiff. The freight boat would sail at four A.M., skiff with the mail at 6 A.M. Other mornings the freight boat would sail at two A.M. The crew of the freight boat consisted of three, except mail day, when it was manned by only two; the third man would have to bring the skiff with the mail, which he considered a soft snap, for usually there would be passengers who assisted in

rowing who had to pay their passage just the same. The stage would be waiting at the foot of [the] lake to convey the mail and passengers over the four miles drive to Minden. Steve mostly went alone, but occasionally I would be sent, and then I would get a good dinner at the Buck Hotel.

The landing at the bottom end of the boat trip was actually at the foot of the Long Arm of Canning Lake, which in those days was considered part of Kashagawigamog. From there, a wagon ride would finish the trip to Minden.

2 · WIGAMOG INN

Wigamog Inn stands on the site of the Gould farm. From 1903 to 1910, Anna Gould, daughter-in-law of Thomas and Isabella Gould (see No. 11 below), welcomed summer visitors to her farmhouse for $3 a night. Everybody was scandalized when she put the price up to $4! All the food on her table—meat, butter, eggs, and produce — came from the farm.

This postcard of the Northern Eagle Inn was mailed on July 30, 1931; postage was 2 cents. Since the cancellation stamp says Allsaw, Ont., and this was the site of the Allsaw post office for many years, the postcard was probably purchased, written, stamped, and franked right here. Photo courtesy Marie Emmerson.

3 · NORTHERN EAGLE

Northern Eagle Tent and Trailer Park began during the First World War as the Northern Eagle Farm Summer Home. The redbrick house on the property, which dates back to the late 1860s or early 1870s, is said to be the oldest brick house in Minden Township outside the village proper. It was built by John Dauncey, who had taken up the land as a Crown grant in 1868 and reputedly traded an arthritic old horse for the bricks. (A horse in any condition would have been worth a house-load of bricks at that time in a countryside where those animals were a rarity; oxen were far more common for hauling and ploughing.) The building soon housed the Allsaw Post Office and did so for many decades.

From 1896 to 1977, with a hiatus from 1905 to 1911, the house and the surrounding land were owned by the Robertson family, who had begun homesteading nearby in 1861. During the war years, from 1914 to 1918, summer visitors started arriving, asking if they might pitch their tents in the fields and could Mrs. Robertson fix their meals? By 1922, they'd talked George Robertson into building the long two-storey addition west of the house and the Northern Eagle Farm Summer Home was born.

During the annual six-week season, from Dominion Day to mid-August when the Canadian National Exhibition in Toronto opened, George and Georgina turned the first floor of the brick house into dining rooms and restricted themselves and their children to the second floor.

After the Second World War, the resort business generally was pushed aside by the cottaging boom and the increasing dominance of the automobile. In 1953, Murray and Helen Robertson (George and Georgina's son and daughter-in-law) closed Northern Eagle. In 1965, however, they reopened as the Northern Eagle Campground, subsequently renaming it Northern Eagle Tent and Trailer Park. In 1992, Northern Eagle was purchased by an association formed by those who had rented lots in the park, some of them for generations.

The old redbrick house remains, despite all these changes, and even holds the record of some of its own history; visitors over the years have scratched their names on its bricks.

4 · INGOLDSBY

Ingoldsby was originally named Austin's Narrows after the Austin family. In 1858, Minden Township was surveyed and, on May 24 of that year, Charles Austin, his wife, and their seven children moved from another property up near Allsaw to homestead here. Austin and his sons built a home of logs taken from the surrounding forest.

Others soon followed, and, by 1862, it was time for a post office. The name Roseneath was proposed, but the government reported that it had been taken by a town farther south between Cobourg and Hastings. The bureaucrats suggested Ingoldsby instead, after a town in Germany.

4A · INGOLDSBY UNITED CHURCH

In 1864, Charles Austin was largely responsible for building a log church, the first in the district, for the Episcopal Methodists. The building was also used as a school for nine months and later housed Branch 1173 of the Orange Lodge.

(It still stands as a storage shed for a cottage on the west side of the narrows.)

In 1884, the congregation began pressing for a new building, but it was four years before construction began on a piece of land donated by Elias and Elizabeth Vinson. This frame structure served for 40 years, when it was replaced by the current brick church. The last service was held in the old building on May 27, 1928, and the cornerstone of the new one was laid on August 10. The service of dedication took place on December 9.

In those days, a fence ran all the way around the church, with a small gate for pedestrians and a large one for horses and Model Ts. An L-shaped drive-shed stood on the northwest corner of the lot, following the present line of spruce trees. In 1962, the back third of the church was added. It cost about $5,000 —as much as the whole building had cost 34 years earlier.

The graves in the cemetery across the road from the church date back to the community's earliest days. Of particular note are the two little stone hearts that hang low to the ground near the fence. They mark the passing in September 1883 of two children: Alberta M. James, who died at the age of five, and Norman

These two stones can still evoke the sorrow that the family of these two little children must have felt.

H. James, presumably her little brother, who died three days later at the age of two years and six months.

The old bridge below Scott's Dam used to carry the Strickland Road (now County Road 1) over the Drag River. The dam is one of many that control water levels throughout the county for the benefit of the Trent-Severn Waterway.

5·FINNISH VILLAGE

The area around the south end of Canning Lake has long been known as the Finnish Village, after the many Finnish families who first came here as summer visitors early in the century. With its birches, rocks, and lakes, the area reminded them of their native land, and so they stayed to become cottagers and run resorts. Their descendants still have homes and cottages here, even to the fourth generation.

One of those resorts was Sunny Rock Lodge, which stood on the west side just below the dam. It was built by Woitto and Alice Konni, who first came to the area to visit to friends in 1915. In 1928, they built a cottage on a huge rock that overlooked the falls. As a Finnish establishment, it of course had a sauna– a rare feature in Haliburton, except in the Finnish Village. In 1934, they hired a fellow Finn, Joseph Tikka, to build the three-storey round-log resort around the cottage. The Konnis ran Sunny Rock Lodge until 1950, when they sold the property to a longtime guest of the lodge. It is now a bed-and-breakfast.

Throughout these years, Murray Robertson of Northern Eagle operated a sightseeing launch, the *Empress of Kushog*. From the late 1930s through the 1940s, Robertson took boatloads of tourists from the lodges all around Kashagawigamog, including his own, on cruises of the lakes. Sunny Rock Lodge was the midtrip stopping point, where passengers could buy tea or soft drinks or chocolate bars before the return trip back up the lakes.

The Miss Haliburton, *owned by Gerry Leboutillier, was one of the sightseeing launches that carried visitors from the resorts on tours around Lake Kashagawigamog during the 1930s and 1940s. Photo courtesy Carol Moffatt.*

6 · COUNTY ROAD 1

This was originally called the Strickland Road, after the lumbering company that built it around 1876 to haul their logs down the valley below the impediment of Ritchie Falls in order to float them south on the Burnt River.

As you turn off the county road towards Ritchie Falls, note the old Victoria Railway bed, which you cross almost immediately. It parallels the county road up to Haliburton and serves as a recreational trail, particularly for snowmobilers.

7 · RITCHIE FALLS

Ritchie Falls is part of the Burnt River, which runs from east of the hamlet of Donald past Kinmount and the town of Burnt River to Cameron Lake. Like all the falls of note in the southern part of the county, the waters tumble over an outcropping of granite in the midst of the surrounding sand and limestone. The road ends in a parking area at the foot of the hill. Walk across the bridge and down along the shore to get a full view.

8 · LOCHLIN

The hamlet of Lochlin began life as Egypt, or maybe Little Egypt, depending on the source. When the Victoria Railway opened in 1878, the name was changed to Ingoldsby Station because it was the closest stop on the rail line to that community. Not that there was a railway station; Gelert had the only station agent between Kinmount and Haliburton. Ingoldsby Station was a flag stop, which meant if you wanted to board the train, you had to flag it down.

It wasn't until the post office was established some time later that the community's name finally became Lochlin. For 25 years, the community had but one postmaster, Levi Pringle, who filled the appointment from his home.

The settlers of Egypt, who were here well before the roads and the railway, rejoiced in decidedly non-WASP names. The birth of John and Louisa Wruth's daughter is said to be recorded in a newspaper clipping of 1866. Eleazar Yerex blazed his own trail into the area in 1872, about the same time Albert Vangesen arrived from Prince Edward County.

8A · LOCHLIN UNITED CHURCH

The first preaching in the Egypt–Lochlin neighbourhood was done by an Episcopal Methodist clergyman named George

Ritchie Falls is one of several splendid waterfalls in the Haliburton Highlands. Granite pushing up through the surrounding sandy soil turns quietly meandering rivers into maelstroms.

Byam. He held services first (and most often) at home of Eleazar Yerex, as well as in other homes and in the schoolhouse.

In 1888, the Lochlin congregation became a part of the Methodist mission run out of Minden, and Albert Vangesen donated a plot of land on the road that would soon be known as Church Road. A frame building modelled on the church at Ingoldsby was put up by two men from Minden named Goodman and Reid. The mission was called "Progress" and was served by the Rev. W.B. Tucker.

By 1925, the 37-year-old frame building was deteriorating badly and it was decided to replace it. Substantial pledges were raised to erect a new church a quarter-mile closer to County Road 1. Land was purchased from Harry McKnight, and a Mr. Schroter of Kinmount was given the construction contract.

The closing service in the old church was held on the last Sunday in May 1925 and the cornerstone of the new brick building was laid on September 4. The new church was the pride of the community. Complete with furnishings, it had cost them just $3,800. Changes have been made to the interior of the church over the years. All the work has been done by voluntary labour, not only by the Lochlin congregation, but by members of the Ingoldsby congregation as well.

8B· LOCHLIN GENERAL STORE

The general store has been a fixture in Lochlin for nearly a hundred years. It was built by the Haliburton Lumber Company around the turn of the century, when they were taking off the pine between Lochlin and Gooderham.

Lois Hill (centre) walks with her friend Shirley Thomson and the dog Lefty in front of her family's general store in Lochlin in 1943. Shirley later married Lois's brother John. The addition to the right of the store provided accommodation for the Hills upstairs and storage for perishables downstairs. The outbuilding at the right provided additional storage. An icehouse originally stood in the space between the two. The girls are approaching the railway tracks in the foreground. The road is behind them on the other side of the fence. Photo courtesy John P. Hill.

In 1907, the 15-acre property was leased by John Stigney Hill and his wife, Mary Vincent, who farmed in the Ingoldsby area; three years later, they bought it.

The store, the outbuildings, and the adjacent boarding house stayed in the Hill family for nearly 60 years. John and Mary's son, Harold, ran the store after he returned from the First World War until his death in 1957. His son Keith followed in his steps until 1968. The store has had several owners since then, but still manages to survive the changing times.

In recent years the fortunes of the Lochlin General Store have fluctuated with the changing economy.

9· DONALD

The ghostly ruins of the old factory stand silent now, but for nearly 40 years in the early part of this century, Donald was the bustling company town of the Standard Chemical Company, which burned hardwood to make charcoal, acetone, wood alcohol, and other by-products.

The story begins in 1908, when R.A. Donald of Markham, owner of the Donald Wood Products Company, established a factory at Dysart Station on the Victoria Railway line and renamed the place for himself. To service the factory, the company built a town: stores, a boarding house, a school, a community centre (known as the Opera House), and homes, which were rented to employees.

In 1915, financial woes forced Donald to sell to Canada Wood Products. They subsequently leased the factory and timber limits to the Standard Chemical Company, which turned it into the largest of their 12 plants. During the First World War, the British War Office contracted to take the factory's entire output.

Thirty-five men worked in the factory itself, running the still house, boilerhouse, kilns, and cooling sheds. Hundreds more worked in the bush, harvesting trees to feed the plant's prodigious appetite. Some of these men came from as far away as Italy, recruited annually as seasonal workers. About half a dozen of the Italians stayed and married. Some brought brides from home; some married local women. Their surnames survive among half a dozen local families. "The Chemical," as the plant was called locally, used a staggering

From its earliest days, the Chemical Factory at Donald was a going concern. This photograph, taken on January 12, 1909, shows not only the extent of the factory buildings, but the massive amounts of cordwood needed to feed its furnaces: 50 cords every 24 hours. The skeletal ruins of the building to the immediate left of the water tower are all that remain today of the entire operation.
Photo courtesy Haliburton Highlands Museum.

amount of wood. The ovens burned red-hot all day and all night, consuming 50 cords every 24 hours. Each cord yielded about 10 gallons of wood alcohol and 30 bushels of charcoal. The acetone, a valuable component of explosives, was shipped to the Canadian Explosives Limited's munitions plant at Nobel, the town north of Parry Sound named after Swedish scientist Alfred Bernhard Nobel, inventor of dynamite and creator of the Nobel Prize.

By the 1940s, the neighbouring timber limits had long since been stripped, and logging operations were now so far afield that expenses were getting out of hand. At the same time, synthetic acetone, which could be made more cheaply, became available. In 1946, under the chairmanship of E.P. Taylor, the plant was closed and dismantled, and the Standard Chemical Company sold its holdings.

Donald was, strictly speaking, a flag stop with a freight shed and a small station to shelter waiting passengers. In fact, the train always stopped here because of the volume of mail to be delivered to the post office in one of the stores. There were two main sidings and a third that was moved about the huge yard in order to transport the piles of cordwood to the plant.

10 · Gould's Crossing

The sign by the road announces the proximity of Gould's Crossing, the last flag-stop on the Victoria Railway before the end of the line at Haliburton. In

1878, Thomas Gould sold 9 of his 99 acres to the Victoria Railway for $180, a goodly profit over the $100 he had originally paid for his whole block of land.

A small building beside the railway track housed a waiting room with a potbellied stove and benches. To catch the train that left Haliburton at 4:30 in the morning, passengers went down to the "station" in the dark, lit a fire, and waited. As the train approached, they went outside and flagged it down with a lantern. It would take them four hours to get to Lindsay, where they had to wait another four hours to catch the train to Peterborough.

11 · Gould Homestead

The homestead of Thomas and Isabella Gould is the oldest log home in the county. The couple (originally from England and Scotland respectively) came in 1864 from Shakespeare, near Stratford, Ontario. They built their first house near the road, but it burned down. Their second house, built in 1867, was also made of logs. It was no more than 24 by 30 feet and only a storey-and-a-half high, yet Isabella and Thomas raised 12 children there.

Although hidden by the additions that have been put on over the years, the 1867 log structure still stands at the heart of the house now occupied by the Goulds' great-granddaughter, Jean Casey, who was born here at Willowbrooke Farm, and her husband, Earle.

CHAPTER SEVEN

CIRCLE TOUR FROM HALIBURTON: ESSONVILLE, WILBERFORCE, TORY HILL, GOODERHAM

Distance: 77 kilometres (46 miles)

The eastern part of Haliburton County has a history all its own. To the usual pursuits of logging and farming were added other wood-related industries and a wide variety of mining enterprises. In days gone by, distance made it difficult to reach the services available in the larger towns. So the people of eastern Haliburton looked to their own resources and came up with their own solutions. This tour takes you through communities that thrive today and some that are now ghost towns.

1 · CHRIST CHURCH, ESSONVILLE

A century ago, the junction of Highway 121 and the Essonville Road (County Road 4) was the centre of the community of Essonville. In 1888, the people who lived on the farms scattered over a 3-mile radius from the intersection decided that, since they already had a post office and a school (built in 1881), it was time for a church.

Christ Church was the first house of worship built in Monmouth Township. It was made of lumber sawn from three pine trees that grew on the site. In addition to the church, there was a rectory on the hill to the west, a log Sunday school to the east (which also served as the Orange Lodge), and a cemetery across the road.

After the Second World War, the economic base of the area shifted east to Wilberforce, and the congregation dwindled. Christ Church was deconsecrated and closed, and, in 1971, the property was deeded to the municipality.

Built in 1888, Christ Church, Essonville, has begun to enjoy a new lease on life.

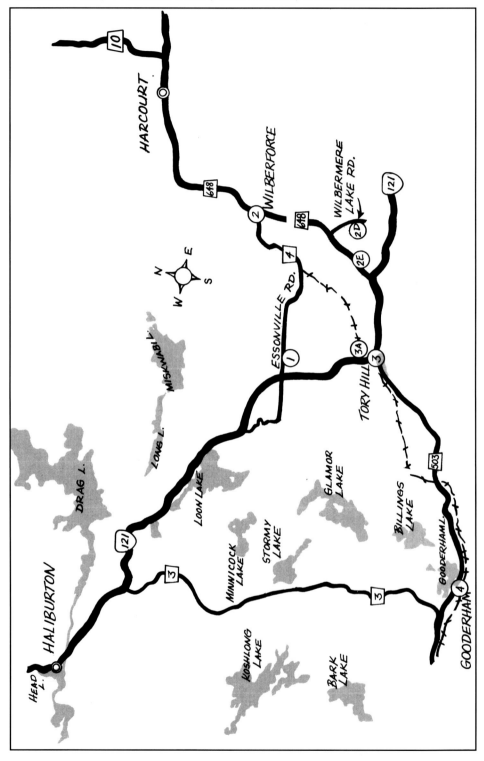

An annual memorial service, held on the Civic Holiday weekend, regularly attracts a hundred or more worshippers. At this service in 1990, it was decided to spend the collection on repairing one of the windows. Under the leadership of Norma Walsh, Margaret Finlay, and Ken Noble (whose grandfather had been a member of the original congregation), this small project quickly snowballed into a major restoration project.

In keeping with the traditions of their ancestors, the people of the community are donating their time, labour, and money to return the church to its original state. Though it is expected that the project will take several more years, Christ Church is already being used more often, particularly at Christmas and for weddings.

2 · WILBERFORCE

This community developed in two parts: South Wilberforce, on the shore of Poverty (now Wilbermere) Lake, where people began settling in the early 1870s, and North Wilberforce, where settlers followed on the heels of the logging companies a decade later. The ascendancy of North Wilberforce was made inevitable by the arrival of the I.B.&O. Railway, which crossed the road near Pusey (now Dark) Lake in the mid-1890s. Before long, the area where the train tracks crossed the road became built up, and the community 2 miles to the south declined.

Lumbering was the major industry until the land was stripped of trees, after which the companies pulled out and left the farmers to subsistence living. In 1937, the Wilberforce Lumber Company, a subsidiary of the Oakville Basket Company, was established. They built a sawmill and a veneer mill to process the logs taken from their 14,500 acres in Dudley Township to the north. In 1948, the company was sold to local interests owned by Jack Wallace and Harold Herlihey, who began producing veneer for the furniture trade. In 1950, the name was changed to the Wilberforce Veneer and Lumber Company. The current operation buys its trees from across Southern Ontario and provides veneer for plywood and furniture.

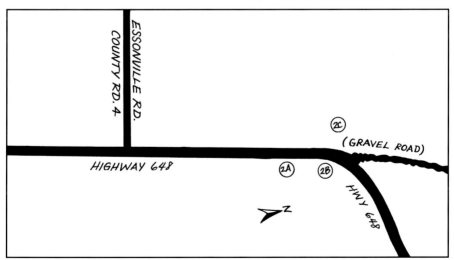

· **WILBERFORCE**

Mining was also a significant enterprise for a time. Diamond Virginia Graphite was the first. From 1910 to 1915, its 50 employees took graphite out of the ground, refined it, and shipped it to Germany. Later on, other entrepreneurs went after molybdenum and uranium, but the ores they found were of inferior grade and none of the ventures was commercially sustainable. The area has since become a mecca for rockhounds, who regularly come in search of more than 60 kinds of minerals and crystals suitable for gemstones.

2A · MARSHALL HOUSE

When the Marshall family first arrived in the area in the early years of the 20th century, they lived for some time in a tent. Their fortunes obviously improved dramatically, because around 1921, Thomas Marshall built this fine stone house on Main Street. When he was appointed postmaster, Marshall added a room at the front of the house to serve as the post office. The Marshalls were also proud owners of the first radio in the area and could count on their friends to drop in whenever there was a hockey game on.

Harold and Beatrice Herlihey bought the Marshalls' house in 1948 and still live there nearly five decades later.

2B · RED CROSS OUTPOST HOSPITAL

The Red Cross Outpost Hospital in Wilberforce was the first such establishment in Ontario. Before it opened in 1922, people needing medical care had to wait for the doctor to arrive on the train, which came through only three times a week. The Monmouth Charitable Association, created specifically for the purpose, bought Alfred Fleming's house on the main street for $650 and stocked it with equipment and supplies provided by Red Cross headquarters in Toronto.

The Red Cross also provided a nurse. The first was a Miss Jackson, who came on a trial basis. Her successors included Gertrude Leroy Miller, Vicki Agnew, and Sylvia Battersby Cameron, who had been born in Essonville to a rector at Christ Church. Like those who serve today in Arctic communities, the nurses at the Outpost Hospital were on their own, making decisions and performing duties left to doctors in larger centres. Fees for patients were set at $1.50 a day; dressings and calls cost $1.

The community was responsible for maintaining the building. Everyone from Gooderham to Highland Grove got involved in raising the funds to keep the hospital open and pay off the mortgage. In the time-honoured fashion still practised today in rural communities, they held picnics, masquerades, dances, ball

Nurses at the Red Cross Outpost Hospital in Wilberforce had to be as intrepid as those who serve today in Arctic communities. Gertude Leroy and a friend's dog named Jack were ready to set out to visit patients around the area on this wintry day in the 1930s. The view looks up Wilberforce's broad main street. The white building on the left (behind her elbow) is St. Margaret's Anglican Church. At the right is the stone Marshall House. The hospital itself is beyond the frame building on the right. Photo courtesy Wilberforce Heritage Guild.

The Outpost Hospital in Wilberforce operated from 1922 to 1963 through the co-operative energies of the Red Cross and the community. In 1991, the community restored the hospital and turned it into a museum.

games, and teas to raise money. They also donated firewood for the stoves and food for the patients.

As roads improved and transportation became easier, the Outpost Hospital was less and less necessary. It closed in 1963 and became the property of the municipality, which rented it as a residence. In 1991, the hospital was restored by the volunteers of the Wilberforce Heritage Guild and reopened as a museum.

2C · St. Margaret's Anglican Church

Until the First World War, the Anglicans of Wilberforce were served by the minister stationed at Christ Church in Essonville. E.G. Robinson was the first clergyman to take up residence in Wilberforce. He held services in homes and schoolhouses and the Orange Lodge, but was constantly on the lookout for more suitable quarters. In 1918, he was

Before it became a house of worship, St. Margaret's Anglican Church was a lumber company bunkhouse.

73

finally able to acquire a two-storey bunkhouse on the main street that had been sold by the Speers and Lauder Lumber Company to Alfred Scholfield. After leading only a few worship services there, however, Robinson was recalled to Toronto.

Fifteen months later, in 1919, a student minister named G.G. Stone took over the charge. He arranged for the purchase of the present site, and the men of the congregation spent two days moving the bunkhouse up the street by winch and rollers.

The upper floor, which had provided sleeping accommodation for the loggers, was removed to create the vault of the nave. The large front and back doors were taken out, and new front and side entrances added. A wood-burning stove was installed for heat and coal-oil lamps for light. Prayer books were brought from Port Hope and furnishings from Cheddar, a vanished town to the east along Highway 121 in Cardiff Township.

The name St. Margaret's may have been selected at a meeting of the church women in 1919. On December 22, 1920, the first service was held in the new church with 53 people in attendance, and the bishop arrived to dedicate it on January 2, 1921.

2D · WILBERFORCE UNITED CHURCH

The one public structure left to mark the community of South Wilberforce is the United church. It was established as Wilberforce Methodist Church in 1889 on land donated by Henry and Isabella Coukell who, six years earlier, had provided the adjacent half-acre for the schoolhouse. The log structure, originally the Methodist church at Kidd's Corners in Cardiff Township, was dismantled, brought here, and rebuilt.

About the turn of the century, the log building was replaced with the current frame structure. It remained unaltered until 1984 when the church received a bequest of $60,000 and used some of the funds to add on a new wing for a Sunday school and a new church hall.

The community cemetery across the road predates the church by ten years. The plaque on the gatepost announces that the first burial took place there in 1879.

2E · HYLAND ICE SUPPLY

Hyland Ice Supply began back up the road on Lake Wilbermere in the days before electricity arrived in the area, when ice provided the means of refrigeration. Starting in 1944, teenager Mel Croft and his friend Gordon Clark spent much of the winter cutting 200-pound blocks of ice out of the lake with a crosscut saw—back-breaking, finger-freezing, life-endangering labour. They then hauled the ice to shore by horse and wagon and packed it in sawdust in an icehouse until summer.

As the ice was needed, Croft and Clark dug it out of the sawdust and drove it back to the lake in a Model A Ford pickup, which they backed into the lake so they could wash off the sawdust by throwing pails of water over the ice. The ice was delivered three times a week to homes and cottages and dairies for their icebox refrigerators.

When electricity arrived in 1947 (the same year that Highway 648 was put through), Croft switched from ice blocks to ice cubes. At the time, the custom of putting ice cubes in drinks was considered quite decadent—like wearing sunglasses, fit only for movie stars and Nevada divorcees. But ice cubes caught on quickly, and Mel and his wife, Bessie, started making their own at their new factory on this site, using water from three wells on the property. Business took off and is still going strong, 50 years after Mel and Gord cut their first block of ice out of Lake Wilbermere.

3 · TORY HILL

There's not much left of Tory Hill these days, though people who live in this sort of community rightly resent hearing their village called a ghost town. But back in the days when it was a tortuous, two-day wagon ride over the hills to Haliburton village, there was plenty of reason to have a bustling town here.

John Anderson came from Apsley in 1881 to serve as the Crown lands agent and postmaster. Anderson was quite the entrepreneur. He owned the first store in town and, in 1893, built a blacksmith's shop, where Cleophis (Clip) Short practised the smithy's trade and sometimes served as village dentist. Anderson also put up a community hall, which served as the courthouse and as the polling station during elections. It was used as well for dances and concerts; Anderson occasionally imported entertainment from Toronto.

The I.B.&O. Railway arrived in Tory Hill in 1895 and the town became the shipping centre for the dozen or more sawmills that operated in the area over the next half-century. At their peak, the mills operated 60 hours a week and the men who worked in them earned an average of 25 cents an hour. Demand was so great at times that in addition to the scheduled thrice-weekly trip to Howland Junction, where the I.B.&O. met the Victoria Railway, a special freight train operated on the off-days to catch up on the backlog of lumber. The town also boasted a cheese factory, which likewise shipped its products out to market on the train.

3A · TORY HILL UNITED CHURCH

The citizens of Tory Hill built themselves a Methodist church in 1903–1904. In 1928, three years after church union, the congregation erected this brick building directly across the road from their first church. When the mortgage was finally burned, Alexander McCrea had the honour of putting the match to it because, as one parishioner put it, if Alex McCrea's part had been taken out, the rest of the church would have fallen down.

At its peak, the congregation of Tory Hill United numbered 25 families, about right for a church seating 80 people. Then, as congregations in both Tory Hill and Wilberforce declined, there was an arrangement for about ten years with Wilberforce United; services were held at Wilberforce in the summer and at Tory Hill in the winter because the latter had an oil furnace. In 1984, however, the Wilberforce congregation received a bequest of $60,000 and decided to go it on their own.

By the mid-1980s, time had finally caught up with Tory Hill United Church. There was no Sunday school by then, and no new families had come into the congregation for some time. One by one, the longtime adherents died and, in the fall of 1988, the church was closed.

The closing of the United church is part of the general decline of Tory Hill, a town there doesn't seem to be a need for anymore. The post office has been gone for some time. The general store closed in 1989. There hasn't been a service station since it was discovered that the fuel tanks were located under the road allowance, and it was going to cost too much to move them.

Tory Hill isn't the only ghost town in Haliburton County, but places like Gelert and Donald and Irondale declined before our time. Tory Hill is different only because it has disappeared before our eyes.

4 · GOODERHAM

The town of Gooderham sprang up at the junction of three transportation routes: the Monck Road (Highway 503), the Buckhorn Road (Highway 507), and the Irondale River. The area was a rich one for the lumbermen; the first licences were issued to Mossom Boyd, J.R. Rodgers, and W.A. Scott. Settlers started moving in around 1870. By 1884, mail service from Kinmount was operating twice a week.

4A · I.B.&O. RAILWAY

The I.B.&O. officially arrived in Gooderham in 1886, adding a fourth means of transportation. It would be another seven years, however, before the community actually had train service.

This odd state of affairs came about because promoters of the railway were to receive bonuses on the basis of a guarantee that the train would reach Gooderham by a certain date in 1886. Unfortunately, they ran out of money and couldn't afford to buy enough track to reach the town. Their solution to the problem was imaginative, if not entirely scrupulous. They ran a train as far as they could, then lifted the rails behind it and laid them down in front of it. By leapfrogging the tracks over the train, they steamed into Gooderham by the required date and received their money. Not until 1893 did the trains actually start running regularly in and out of Gooderham.

The last train pulled out of the Gooderham station on March 31, 1960. The tracks were pulled up shortly afterwards and sold to make razor blades.

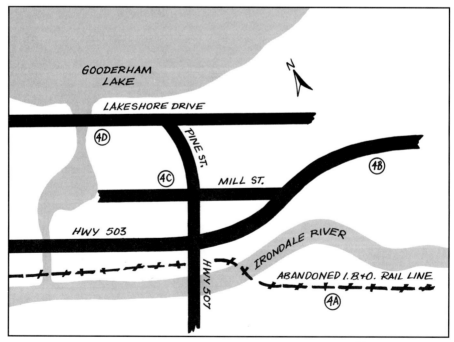

GOODERHAM LAKE

LAKESHORE DRIVE

N

4D

PINE ST.

4C

MILL ST.

4B

HWY 503

HWY 507

IRONDALE RIVER

ABANDONED I.B.+O. RAIL LINE

4A

· GOODERHAM

The falls at Gooderham powered the Hunter family's sawmill for over a hundred years. By the early 1960s, it was one of the few water-powered mills still operating in Canada. The mill burned down in the late 1970s.

4B · GOODERHAM UNITED CHURCH

The Methodist mission arrived in Gooderham in 1874 as part of the circuit out of Minden. Services were held in a log school that stood a quarter of a mile east of the present church. It eventually burned down and was rebuilt next door to the present church; this building is now privately owned.

The land for the church was donated by Solomon and Adelaide Hadley, and, in a local expression of the familiar story, the building was erected by community labour out of lumber sawn at Hunter's Mill. There was also a 70-foot drive-shed for housing the horses that brought the faithful to worship; it was taken down in 1930. Gooderham's new Methodist church held its opening services in 1894. In 1905, pews were bought from a church in Little Britain to replace the plank benches.

Although it had long been felt that it was too small, the building remained unchanged until 1960. The problem of whether to rebuild or add on was compounded by the fact that the Department of Highways kept taking slices off the front yard to widen the highway. It was finally decided to build a new foundation a full building width to the east and a full length to the south, farther away from the road.

The original building was moved onto the new foundation; the Department of Highways even chipped in with a contribution towards the cost of moving the building. The basement was finished to provide the space needed for Sunday school and social events. The added distance to the road made it possible to build a vestibule on the front.

However, much in the reconstituted church of 1961 remained the same as it had been since 1894. Even the original coal-oil lamps were still in use because it would be a few more years before electricity arrived in Gooderham. There was no running water for the kitchen in the basement until 1987, when a well was dug. Even the privy out back served its purpose until then.

4C · BARR'S GENERAL STORE

Barr's General Store has been run by four generations of the same family. Towards the end of the last century, merchant Peter Barr moved from Irondale to Gooderham to take advantage of the town's growth as a lumbering centre. In 1895, he built the house beside the current store and, in the front room behind the big window, ran a general store. Around the turn of the century, he built Barr's General Store.

His son, also named Peter, took over from his father and ran the store until he died from influenza in his early forties. His son Gordon Barr, only 16 years old at the time, took up the challenge of the family business and ran it until 1960, when his son Ron became the owner and operator. Like his father and grandfather before him, Ron also became the town's funeral director. Thirty-five years later, he still fills both roles.

This combination of businesses harks back to earlier times, when the funeral director was called the undertaker. Barr's store once had a sign outside that proclaimed "Furniture, Feed, Groceries, and Coffins for Sale," and the second floor was set aside for casket display. In those days, there were no funeral homes, and deceased family members, once they were embalmed, would be

Barr's General Store (on the right) was one of the buildings dominating Gooderham's main street. The date on the note on the back of the postcard is January 14, 1903.
Photo courtesy Carol Moffatt.

laid out in the front parlour. People would come in to Barr's and buy their own coffins, take them home, and line them with the wood of their choice. The coffin would then be put away until it was needed.

4D · HUNTER'S MILL

In the mid-1870s, Isaac and John Hunter came from Kinmount and built a combined grist and saw mill at these falls. At last, settlers could have their oats, wheat, and corn ground locally instead of having to haul them to Minden. The mill burned down in the mid-1890s and only the sawmill was rebuilt by John Hunter, his son Jack, and his nephew Lorne. When John Sr. died in the early 1900s, his widow took over and for 30 years the firm was known as Alice Hunter and Sons.

The Hunter Mill continued to operate well into the second half of this century. By the early 1960s, it was one of the few water-powered mills still in operation in Canada. From 1968, when Murray Hunter, one of Alice's great-grandsons, took it over, the mill was cutting 3 million to 4 million board feet annually.

Hunter's Mill closed in February 1975. Two years later, after the family had failed to persuade the township to preserve it as an historic site, they decided to tear it down. While this was going on, vandals set what was left on fire and it burned to the ground.

CHAPTER EIGHT

CIRCLE TOUR FROM HALIBURTON: WEST GUILFORD, EAGLE LAKE, FORT IRWIN, HARBURN

Distance: 61 kilometres (37 miles)

While most of the population of Canada seems huddled towards its southern edge, some of the most beautiful and dramatic places are to be found to the north. Such is also the case in Haliburton County. The communities of West Guilford, Eagle Lake, and Fort Irwin are three gateways to the farther reaches of the county.

1 · WEST GUILFORD

The village of West Guilford grew up where the road from the Maple Lake settlement to the west grazed the southern shore of Pine Lake. (The route to Haliburton was no better than a bush trail for several decades.)

This community was once a hotbed of horse-racing. From 1909 to 1925, George Barry held summertime sulky and saddle races on a half-mile track at his farm. Crowds and competitors came from as far away as Lindsay and Fenelon Falls. Barry kept several good mounts himself; the most famous was a trotter he named Guilford Boy.

Over half a dozen years, Guilford Boy collected a trunkful of trophies and ribbons for Barry and his trainer, Jimmy Powell, at races and fall fairs across the province. One season, they took him to the United States, where he broke several track records. Guilford Boy's career ended when he was kicked on his hind leg by another horse and died from the resulting infection.

West Guilford is the birthplace of another famous athlete: Bernie Nichols of the National Hockey League.

The Grass River, one of the many sections of the Gull River, meanders from Pine Lake (in the background) through the community of West Guilford.

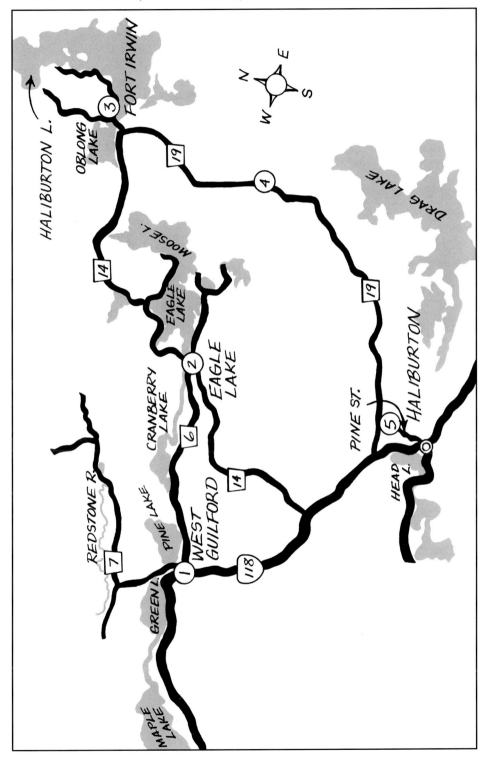

*St. Andrew's Anglican Church was built in 1931 on land donated by Mark and Sarah Jane Sisson.
In 1989, their 12 surviving children commissioned stained-glass windows from Minden artist Wendy
Ladurantaye to be installed above the altar in their parents' memory.*

1A · St. Andrew's Anglican Church

St. Andrew's Anglican Church was built in 1931, but the church registers date back to 1919, when the congregation worshipped in the Orange Hall in return for maintaining the propane lamps.

Nelson Barnum had his home and store and the first post office in West Guilford on land that stretched along the south shore of Pine Lake. In 1906, he gave some of that land to his daughter Sarah Jane and her husband, Mark Sisson, and they took over the store and the post office. In 1931, the couple donated the property where they had their gardens for the church.

The building cost $1,700—a not inconsiderable sum in the dark days of the Depression when the weekly collection might yield only a dollar or two. Nonetheless, the congregation managed to pay off the debt within a year. The St. Andrew's Women's Auxiliary had been formed in 1930 and their fundraising efforts were undoubtedly critical in erasing the debt.

Because the church lacked a basement, there was no place to hold church suppers or other social events. The solution was both simple and unique. Four doors were put across the front of the sanctuary; when they were closed, the nave became the church hall.

In 1942, the basement was dug out. In the 1950s, the church was remodelled again, and in the 1960s, a church hall was added behind the sanctuary to house the Sunday school and the nursery. However, the addition blocked up the windows over the altar and it took a few years to figure out how to solve the problem. In 1989, the 12 surviving children of Mark and Sarah Jane Sisson commissioned Minden artist Wendy Ladurantaye to create three stained-glass windows, artificially lit from behind, in memory of their parents.

1B·WEST GUILFORD BAPTIST CHURCH

Contrary to the notion that interdenominational coldness was common in the 19th century, there was much cooperation and interaction among pioneer congregations. Many elderly residents of West Guilford can remember going to both the Anglican and Baptist services each Sunday. After all, there wasn't much else the faithful were allowed to do on a Sunday, and, with the singing and the preaching, it was good entertainment.

Families even crossed denominational lines, as the story of the Baptist church in West Guilford, the first church to be built in the township, makes clear. For, like St. Andrew's, it owes its origins to the Barnum family.

It was Charles, one of Nelson's brothers, who was the Baptists' benefactor. He owned land on the north side of Pine Lake and donated some of it for the church site. Charles's wife, Jane, had a brother, Dr. Albert Thomas Sowerby, who was a Baptist minister. When he came to spend holidays with his sister, Sowerby would preach at the schoolhouse. As a result, he built up a local following for the Baptist persuasion.

In 1905, Charles and Jane Barnum donated the land for a church. The lot was large enough to accommodate a cemetery — to this day the only one in the township. The church was finished in 1906 — built, as usual, by voluntary labour. Sowerby's involvement continued: he arranged for financial support from other Baptist congregations and furnished the church with chairs, pulpit, organ, and a silver communion set. As a result, the new church was able to open free of debt.

In 1925, the church was struck by lightning; it was Charlie Barnum who spotted the fire and put it out. In 1927, the front entranceway, facing the lake, was reoriented to the west side of the building to make more room for the

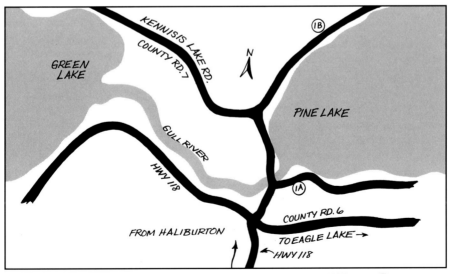

· WEST GUILFORD

driveway. During the Second World War, electricity replaced the gas lamps, which had in their turn replaced the original oil lamps. In 1951, the chairs were replaced with pews from Clarence-ville Baptist Church in Quebec.

A few years ago, the congregation was aging and it seemed as though the church might close. But an influx of young families has brought new life into the church and its future looks secure.

SIDE TRIP

The road that leads through the small business district of West Guilford continues on through beautiful hilly country to Kennisis Lake, named for Joe Caneese, an Algonquian patriarch of the last century whose family had lived there for many generations.

2 · EAGLE LAKE

The pretty settlement of Eagle Lake grew where the lake of the same name flows into the upper reaches of the Gull River. It was the focus of farming families who came to settle in the area starting in the 1860s and 1870s. Guilford was one of the nine townships belonging to the Canadian Land and Emigration Company, and it was through the company and its subsidies that many people came from Great Britain to these hills.

2A · EAGLE LAKE SCHOOL

When the International Cooperage opened for business, the population of Eagle Lake grew quickly. By the late 1930s, the overflow of students from the 1892 log school was being bused daily to West Guilford. Eventually, it was decided that a larger school was needed in Eagle Lake. This brick building, completed in 1945, had two large classrooms (40 feet long by 22 feet wide with 12-foot ceilings) on the main floor; at the end of one classroom was a raised stage so the room could double as an auditorium. The basement provided two gymnasiums (one for the boys and one for the girls) and two changing areas.

The Eagle Lake School offered grades one to eight. When the roster topped 100 students, grades seven and eight were once again transferred to West Guilford. After the Cooperage moved out, families started moving away. Enrolment declined and the school finally closed in 1972. A decade later, it became a private home.

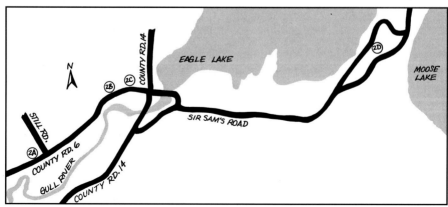

· EAGLE LAKE

INTERNATIONAL COOPERAGE

In 1932, extensive tracts of timber in the neighbouring townships of Harburn and Eyre were purchased by Dominion Cooperage, later International Cooperage of Canada Limited, a Canadian subsidiary of an American barrel-making concern. The firm established a heading mill at the foot of Eagle Lake to manufacture "heads," the round tops and bottoms of barrels. Facilities included a boiler house, an engine room, a sawmill (or green side), a kiln (or dry side), drying sheds, a pumphouse, and a warehouse.

At its peak, the Cooperage provided year-round employment for an average of 60 men, who worked from 7:00 A.M. to 6:00 P.M. every day to turn 14,000 to 16,000 board feet of lumber into barrel heads. The heads were then shipped to a sister plant in Wiarton, where the staves were made and the barrels and kegs assembled.

Fires in 1935 and 1940 destroyed the plant, but the operation was sufficiently profitable that it was rebuilt and expanded both times. By the early 1950s, though, the profits were no longer there; the Cooperage ceased operations in 1954 and the buildings were demolished. The American company, now called Greif Containers, still holds 30,000 acres of land in Guilford and adjacent townships.

2B · BOLENDER'S QUARRY

In 1948, Percy Bolender and his sons closed down their quarrying operations in Lochlin and Wilberforce, and opened White Star Mines in Eagle Lake to take dolomite out of the ground. This white mineral runs underneath the drainage basin of the Gull River and has mitigated the severest effects of acid rain in the lakes and rivers downstream. Industrially, dolomite is used in stucco, roofing granules, precast concrete, and other conglomerate building materials.

Although the company (now controlled by other interests) still owns the quarry, the five-minute warning whistle prior to a blast has not been heard in several years.

At its peak in the 1930s and 1940s, the International Cooperage in Eagle Lake provided employment for 60 men. The moose strolling past the main mill in this photograph had just finished taking a bath in the hot pond, where ice was thawed out of logs before sawing.
Photo courtesy Brant Sisson.

2C · EAGLE LAKE COMMUNITY CHURCH

In 1937, Mrs. Lewis Pritchard, assisted by Mrs. Hathaway, put on a Ten Cent Tea at her home to raise money to buy whitewash for the walls of the cookhouse at the International Cooperage, where church services were then held. The women who came to tea that afternoon agreed that it was time they had a proper church.

The women's initiative was subsequently taken up by three men: Fred Greer, who managed the Cooperage, Lewis Pritchard, who had a logging operation, and W.O. Bailey, who had a sawmill. These three men put up the money and materials for the church. Most of the labour was donated by the men who worked at the Cooperage;

they came regularly after work and then again after supper to put up the building.

Right from the beginning, it was intended that the church be nondenominational. However, it has always had a Baptist minister because only the Baptist minister could fit in a service on Sunday morning.

Changes to the building over the ensuing decades have been minimal. The huge woodstove in the basement, for instance, which had so many pipes coming out of it that it was called "the octopus," was replaced in 1961 with an oil furnace. Stained-glass windows were also installed — which meant the congregation could no longer see the occasional moose wandering by. The tapestries on the walls are the work of Eagle Lake women.

2D · SIR SAM'S INN

In 1916 and 1917, at the height of the First World War, Sir Sam Hughes, Canada's Minister of Militia and Defence and the Member of Parliament for the riding of Victoria–Haliburton, found time to amass a tract of 2,000 acres on the east side of Eagle Lake.

Sam called his retreat Glen Eagle and had a 14-bedroom country home erected in the style of a European hunting lodge. Sam was well thought of by his constituents, who elected him at every opportunity but one from 1896 to 1916. He enhanced his reputation locally by bringing a one-man economic boom to Eagle Lake. In addition to the land he purchased by Bargain and Sale (either for back taxes or as a result of defaults on mortgages), he acquired several lots

When Sir Sam Hughes, Canada's Minister of Militia and Defence, built a retreat on the shores of Eagle Lake in 1917, he brought a one-man economic boom to the community. The European-style hunting lodge was restored in 1979 and opened as Sir Sam's Inn.

The hills of the Eagle Lake area offer fine downhill skiing. Sir Sam's Ski Area has been in operation since 1965 on part of the 2,000-acre tract Sir Sam Hughes amassed nearly 50 years earlier. A ski chalet, quad lifts, and snow-making equipment help make it a first-class facility.

from farmers who were glad to take the money and retire or continue as tenant farmers.

Sam hired local men to build Glen Eagle and, when it was completed, engaged local women to act as maids and cooks and nannies. The fields and gardens of his tenant farmers provided food for the kitchen and feed for the stables. Sam gave each farmer a cow and a team of horses to use when they weren't needed on the big farm. He also arranged for a private telephone line, the first in the area.

Sam enjoyed the sanctuary of Glen Eagle for only a few years, until his death in August 1921. His widow and then his children kept the estate until 1945, when it was sold to local residents. In 1965, the property came into the hands of a group of developers, who created Sir Sam's Ski Area, the county's only downhill skiing facility. Fourteen years later, they sold the house itself,

along with 12 acres, to James and Liz Orr, who turned Glen Eagle into a resort that still bears its creator's name.

3·FORT IRWIN

The first white people to come to the narrows where Haliburton Lake flows south into Oblong Lake were loggers. The community takes its name from lumberman James M. Irwin. In 1877, Irwin became a partner of Bobcaygeon-based lumber baron Mossom Boyd, whose company was already logging timber limits in the area. Boyd's local depot camp stood on the flat piece of land at the north end of Oblong Lake opposite the road.

Fort Irwin still seems like the end of the line. In fact, it is the gateway to a whole new part of cottage country.

Cottage development took a different turn on Haliburton Lake than in most other parts of the county. Elsewhere, a farmer whose land included some shoreline would sell off lots as the spirit, or financial necessity, moved him. Lakefront property could provide a farming family with a much needed pension fund. Property for sale was advertised by word of mouth. People interested in buying made their deals directly with the owner, without benefit of real estate agents. Even the surveying was pretty casual at times.

Cottage development around Haliburton Lake was more controlled. The story begins in the early 1950s with a Peterborough lawyer named James Dunn. Dunn and his partner, builder Jack Hayward, had been speculating in real estate and house-building in Peterborough when a housing slump hit and they lost everything. Dunn's reaction was to go on a two-week bender. When he got home, one of the few things he remembered was a late-night conversation in Eagle Lake.

Passing through Eagle Lake late one evening, Dunn had seen a light and stopped to ask if he could rent a room for the night. The man of the house offered him a coffee and the two got talking. The man from Eagle Lake proceeded to tell Dunn how to make a million dollars by developing lakefront lots for cottagers. Dunn went back to Peterborough and talked the idea over with Hayward. Together they formed the Haliburton Development Company. Dunn and Hayward made an arrangement with Clayton Wesley Hodgson, who owned sizable tracts of land around the lake from which he cut timber for his sawmill on the shore. Each time Hodgson released a lot to the Peterborough partners, they paid him $2 a foot. (Better known as C.W., Hodgson served as the riding's Member of Parliament from 1945 to 1963.)

Dunn and Hayward drew up three basic cottage plans and sold the rough building along with the lot for $2,250 to $2,750. Customers would choose their lot and then decide which cottage plan they wanted put up. Hayward purchased the building materials from Peterborough and Haliburton and hired local tradesmen to do the building. The customers could then finish off the interior in their own style. In the decades since, a number of these cottages have been transformed into permanent homes, and other homes and cottages have been built on the lakes still farther north and east.

THE BIGGEST PINE

To the east of Haliburton Lake, in a valley near the eastern edge of Harburn Township, accessible only by a rough trail, stands the biggest pine tree in the province. Not the tallest—that honour goes to a white pine near Blind River—but by a combination of height and girth, the biggest.

At 150 feet high (about half the height of Toronto's City Hall) and 20 feet around, this white pine gives some idea of what the forests of Ontario must have looked like before the loggers arrived. Its age has been estimated at 350 to 400 years, which places its first sprouting sometime between 1590 and 1640.

Several factors have preserved the tree. Because it is in a valley, it has been protected from lightning. Because the main trunk splits in two about 35 feet up, perhaps the result of an attack in the distant past by the white pine weevil, it was considered defective by the loggers. And notwithstanding the split, it was just too big, even 125 years ago, for the loggers to be able to get it out.

Greif Containers, on whose land it stands, is an enthusiastic protector of the tree because it provides a vital seed source for natural reforestation. They are now cutting the fifth and sixth generation of the seedlings from Ontario's biggest tree.

Harburn Township is home to the biggest tree in Ontario. The split partway up the trunk may be the result of an attack in the distant past by the white pine weevil. Photo courtesy Lila Watt Austin.

4 · HARBURN

The history books have little to say about Harburn, perhaps because the story echoes in so many ways what was happening elsewhere, and because there is nothing left to mark the settlement's existence. Only those who grew up here—though they've since moved away and are advancing in years—would be able to tell one stretch of forest from the next.

Harburn Township was one of the nine belonging to the Canadian Land and Emigration Company. It was surveyed in 1862 and settlers began arriving soon afterwards, travelling up this long bush road from Haliburton village. The loggers were here too: Mossom Boyd had exclusive cutting rights.

Harburn's first school was established in 1872, which implies the presence of enough families to provide children for classes. Church services were held in the Orange Hall. In addition to worship, services provided an opportunity for the community and its scattered families to get together once a week, in spite of narrow roads of dubious passability at many times of the year.

Harburn was renowned as a hotbed of Orange sentiment. On July 12, 1690, English and Irish Protestant forces led by William of Orange, King of England, had defeated the Irish Catholics at the River Boyne in Ireland. For 250 years thereafter, members of the Orange Lodge paraded every July 12 to commemorate the event.

On one "Glorious Twelfth," Harburn resident Curly Bill Roberts took his seven sons to Lindsay and won a prize—a bag of first-grade flour—for being the Orangeman with the most sons present who were also members. The prize was put to excellent use by his wife, Lydia Wylie Roberts, who was renowned for her skills as a cook. (Curly Bill and Lydia must have had a lot of mouths to feed: their children provided them with 53 grandchildren.)

To the east of the Harburn settlement is the geological phenomenon known locally as the Harburn Wells, or the Natural Wells. Within walking distance of the site of the old Harburn School are several potholes, smooth circular depressions about 12 feet across and 10 feet deep. They are thought to have been created by the swirling waters of a melting glacier at the end of the ice age 10,000 years ago. Because the wells are now on private land, few people have been able to see them in recent years.

5 · HALIBURTON CEMETERIES

Evergreen Cemetery, on the right, is the Protestant cemetery. The land was bought by the municipality in 1870. Alexander Niven surveyed the cemetery and laid out the plots. In 1878, he purchased the first plot, although he would not need it for another 33 years.

The congregation of St. Anthony's Roman Catholic Church established the cemetery on the left in the late 1930s, about the same time they built the church. The first graves date from 1943.

An autumn canopy hovers over the quiet back stretches of the Harburn Road, which once threaded together a community of farms between Haliburton village and Fort Irwin. Now only those who grew up here would be able to tell one stretch of forest from the next.

CHAPTER NINE

CIRCLE TOUR:
STANHOPE TOWNSHIP

Distance: 60 kilometres (36 miles)

Some of the most dramatic and popular scenic sights in the county are to be found in Stanhope Township. So is some of the finest historical architecture. This roundabout tour of the township extends from the village of Carnarvon at its southern boundary north to the edge of the wilderness in our own backyard.

1·PETERSON ROAD

East and West Roads are among the few remnants of the Peterson Road, one of the colonization roads built by Upper Canada to encourage the spread of settlement. Named after Joseph S. Peterson, who surveyed the route, it was originally designed to go from Ottawa to Georgian Bay. The portion from the Muskoka River to the Madawaska River was completed by 1863, but like the Monck Road farther south, the Peterson Road was never well maintained, and, within 20 years, the wilderness had reclaimed most of it. Only in 1969 was Highway 118 put through to provide a direct route from Muskoka to Haliburton.

2·ZION UNITED CHURCH

Zion United began in 1891 as Zion Methodist Church. The Minute Book of the congregation, still in the possession of a descendant of one of the founders, records the decisions and actions taken from January of that year through the first 15 years of the church.

On February 2, 1891, the Minute Book reports, logs for the rafters and studs were cut in Phoebe Damion's woods (see No. 6 below) by the men of the congregation and sawn into lumber at the sawmill up at Buckslide (or Buck's Slide, as it was then known, after Daniel Buck, who built wooden slides to carry

Buckslide is one of several beautiful waterways in Stanhope Township.

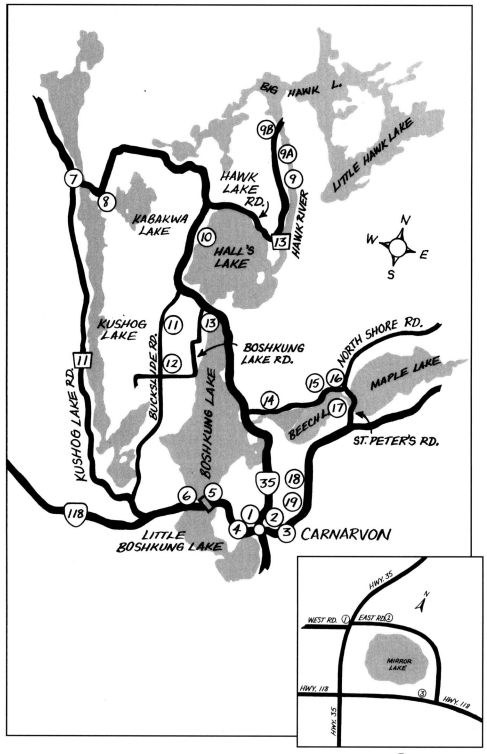

logs from Kushog to Boshkung Lake). On February 12, trees on Joseph Hopkins's land were felled for foundation timbers and hewn square with broad axes.

When Zion Methodist (later United) Church was built in 1891, it lacked the distinctive spire over the front entrance. That was added after a fire caused by lightning in 1962. Photo courtesy Carol Moffatt.

In May, the men of the community were called away to fight a spate of brushfires and so a carpenter, Louis MacDonald, was hired to finish the building. The men got back in time to put the shingles on the roof.

All this time, the women had been holding teas and concerts in order to raise money towards the cost of construction. Everyone's efforts culminated in the dedication of the new church on September 13, 1891.

In 1921, the people from Twelve Mile Presbyterian Church (see Chapter 4, No. 4) joined the flock of Zion Methodist to form one congregation. In 1934, a stone basement was added under the church. The Christian Education wing was added in 1961.

Lightning set the church on fire in July 1962. It struck the pump at a neighbouring house, ran through the battery charger in yet another neighbour's garage, and leapt to the front of the church. There was no organized volunteer fire department

in those days—whoever had a pump and a motor to run it showed up. Water to fight the fire was pumped up from Mirror Lake on the other side of the road. When the smoke had cleared, considerable damage had been done to the south end of the building. Fortunately, the insurance money allowed the congregation to build a new spire and front entrance.

Immediately to the east of the church lie the remnants of the original north-south road. Depending on where you were headed, it was called the Beech Lake Road, the Hall's Lake Road, or the Minden Road. It was eventually supplanted when Highway 35 was built, which explains the jog in the highway and why Carnarvon sits beside the highway, rather than astride it.

The general store in Carnarvon dates back over a century. It has survived three fires that repeatedly destroyed the adjacent house, which was rebuilt each time. Photo courtesy Carol Moffatt.

3 · GENERAL STORE

A general store stood on this site for over a century. In 1898, George P. Hart purchased the existing business from Joseph Hopkins and added the post office to the operation. T.H. Rogers and his son Clayton ran both the store and the post office from 1907 to 1944. Clayton Rogers later went into politics and became reeve of the municipality of Anson, Hindon, and Minden. Over the years, more than one fire destroyed the adjacent house, but the store remained intact. The building continues to house the post office, but the general store has been replaced by a beauty salon.

4 · HARRISON'S WOODS

Lifelong Carnarvon resident Ross Harrison donated this 20-acre woodlot to the province in 1975. Before handing the property over, he laid out a short nature and hiking trail through the woods. Its course follows portions of the old Peterson Road (see No. 1 above), now almost buried in the undergrowth. The property is managed for public use by the Ministry of Natural Resources, which also provides a one-page handout on the trail and maintains a small parking lot beside the highway.

A short, pleasant nature and hiking trail meanders through Harrison's Woods.

5 · DAMION'S BRIDGE

The original wooden bridge that spanned the narrows between Boshkung Lake to the right and Little Boshkung Lake to the left was condemned as unsafe in 1912. Nonetheless people chose to continue using it, rather than take a detour of several miles. The story goes that one day, when a farmer was walking a newly bought cow home across the rickety bridge, the timbers gave out and the two got a dunking. As a result, the old bridge was finally torn out and replaced.

When it was rebuilt again in 1969, it was named Damion's Bridge in recognition of the contributions Phoebe Ann Damion had made to the community (see No. 6 below).

6 · MOOREFIELD ACRES

The flat stretch of land on the north side of the highway at the west end of Damion's Bridge was first cleared by the Algonquians, members of the Ojibwa Nation. Here they cultivated corn, beans, squash, potatoes, and tomatoes—all foods unknown to Europeans when they arrived in North America. By the time settlers arrived in this area, however, most of the Algonquians were long gone, sent to the reserve at Rama on Lake Couchiching in accordance with treaties signed in 1815 and 1848.

After the aborted Upper Canada Rebellion of 1837, Isaac Hunter, one of the rebels, fled with his wife to the Burnt River area, where they lived by hunting and trapping. By 1852, Hunter's first wife had died and the settlement had become too populous for his taste. So he loaded his canoe once more and headed farther north, coming to rest here in the clearing at the narrows. By 1866, the press of settlement was pushing Hunter and his family still farther north, this time to the end of the Bobcaygeon Road at the Oxtongue River, just south of Dwight.

When Isaac Hunter moved north, George Mason took over his 114 acres at the narrows as a free grant from the Crown. In 1871, Mason sold it to Alfred S. and Phoebe Ann Moore. Alfred died only three years later of tuberculosis and Phoebe married Charles Damion. But he proved to be an unsuitable husband, and Phoebe soon sent him packing.

Phoebe Damion was a driving force in the area: she became the postmaster, started a cheese factory, and ran a boarding house that provided accommodation for schoolteachers, circuit ministers, loggers, travelling salesmen, and tourists. In 1897, she sold the property to her son and daughter-in-law, Alfred Walter and Louisa J. Moore.

In 1904, Robert Irvin Moore (no relation) bought the property, named the house Moorefield Lodge, and continued to run it as a boarding and tourist home. In 1930, Moore sold the farm to Clayton Percival Rogers, owner of the general store. The property still belongs to members of the Rogers family. Robert Bateman, the wildlife artist, and his brothers, Jack and Ross, spent their childhood summers at a Boshkung Lake cottage on the Rogers' farm. All three Batemans still have cottages in the area.

Part of Ox Narrows Lodge was said to have been the cookhouse of the nearby road camp during the construction of Highway 35 in the 1930s. This postcard advertised the lodge in its later heyday. Photo courtesy Carol Moffatt.

7 · OX NARROWS

This narrowing of Kushog Lake has been called Ox Narrows since sometime in the last century, when a team of oxen drowned here. Most settlers had travelled up the colonization road in carts drawn by teams of oxen, with all their worldly goods loaded in the wagon and their children perched on top. Consequently oxen were far more common than horses in pioneering days; they would not become a novelty until this century.

Ox Narrows Lodge was built in the late 1930s. Legend has it that the main lodge was originally, in part at least, the cookhouse for the road camp. When construction in this area was finished and the construction crew moved on, the cook is said to have claimed squatter's rights to the building, quit the crew, and stayed here. Some of the cabins along the lakeshore were originally used to house the labourers who built this part of Highway 35.

If you have enough time, turn left at Highway 35 and drive 7 1/2 miles north to Dorset (see Chapter 10). Otherwise, turn right at Highway 35.

8 · KANAWA CANOE MUSEUM

The world's most comprehensive collection of canoes began here, adjacent to Camp Kandalore. Under the leadership of Kirk Wipper, a professor at the

University of Toronto and one of Kandalore's owners, the collection grew to include nearly 600 irreplaceable canoes, kayaks, and rowboats from around the world. During summers between 1974 and 1978, a specially designed two-storey log building was erected to house the boats.

The collection remained here at the Kanawa Canoe Museum until 1995, when it was taken over by the newly formed Canadian Canoe Mu-seum and moved to Peterborough. The museum's board hopes that the move to a larger centre and affiliation with Trent University will enable them to raise funds for a new building, ensure the safety of the collection, and make the collection more accessible for research. The Canadian Canoe Museum opened officially in Peterborough in May 1996.

9 · HAWK RIVER

The stream flowing beside the road is known officially as the Kennisis River and locally as the Hawk River. Two picnic areas between the road and the river are maintained by the municipality for day use by the public.

9A · HAWK RIVER LOG CHUTE

The top of the dam provides the perfect vantage point for a good view of the historic Hawk River log chute. Such chutes were important in the river drives that took the logs from the top of the watershed south to mill and to market.

When logs carried downwards at high speed by the power of a waterfall struck large rocks, they were likely to pile up in logjams, which were dangerous and expensive to break up. In addition, the ends of the logs would split or "broom back" when they hit the rocks. This dam-age made them less valuable as timber because they then had to be cut into shorter lengths of lumber. The chute, therefore, protected both the logs and the loggers' profits.

This log chute is the third to be constructed here. The first one was built sometime between 1861, when the first timber licences were issued in Stanhope Township, and the turn of the century. It was probably constructed by the Gull River Company of Coboconk, one of the companies with cutting rights in the area. Over the years, the wooden structure deteriorated. It was rebuilt in 1948 by the Hall's Lake Lumber Company. In the decades that followed, however, trucks became the sole mode of transporting logs and the river drives were discontinued. Once again, the Hawk River log chute fell into disrepair.

In the late 1960s, the council of Stanhope Township decided to reconstruct the chute to commemorate the role that the logging industry played in the history of the Highlands. The structure was recreated in 1971 using timber cut at Elgin Stouffer's mill near Hall's Lake. In some places, the new timbers were set on top of existing square-cut logs that had remained intact.

Elvin Johnson acted as job superintendent. Fittingly, he and a number of the other men who worked on the project were descendants of pioneers of the region who had depended so much on logging for their livelihoods.

9B · BIG HAWK LANDING

Big Hawk Landing is a jumping-off point for cottagers on the Hawk Lakes, which are accessible for the most part only by boat. There is a store at the landing, should you be looking for some refreshment and a safe place to turn around.

10 · COOPER HOUSE

This beautiful stone house is the work of stonemason John Henry Billing, who also built St. Peter's Anglican Church (see No. 17 below). He built this house for Emma Wyatt, one of his wife's three sisters, and her husband, James Cooper.

11 · ST. STEPHEN'S ANGLICAN CHURCH

This stone church is most renowned for not having been built by John Henry Billing.

At the turn of the century, the local congregation approached Billing to erect their church. The master stonemason is thought to have designed it, but when the time came to build, he was busy with another project and could not begin work as quickly as the congregation would have liked. After several months of waiting, George Hewitt, who lived with his family in the stone house across the road, decided to get the project started by excavating the basement and building the foundation with the assistance of his four sons.

When Billing arrived to begin work, he declared the quality of construction not up to his standard and refused to proceed with the rest of the church unless the foundation was removed. Hewitt likewise refused to budge, and so Billing walked away from the contract. Anyone who has had the opportunity to compare the basement walls of St. Peter's and St. Stephen's would have to agree with Billing's decision.

Construction of St. Stephen's became a community project. But more facts are hard to come by because the early church records went missing a long time ago. One version of the story says that a stonemason named King was working on the Hewitt house at the time of this controversy and that he supervised the congregation in constructing the church.

Years ago, when the road was level with the churchyard, it used to be possible to drive in through the iron gates between the two arches. Behind the church stood a drive shed to accommodate horses and wagons. The two-hole privy still stands against the southeast corner of the building, partly overgrown by a raspberry bush.

The first low stone pillar to the north of the church was matched by a second one erected farther north in 1984 in memory of Ethel Moore Harrison, who, with her husband, Ben, owned the adjacent farm and donated the land for the cemetery extension. The land for the church was originally donated by Thomas Godwin, who is buried in the churchyard.

In the middle of this century, the size of the congregation began dwindling— a trend that never reversed itself. In 1991, St. Stephen's closed its doors.

12 · BOSKUNG SCHOOL

This was the third school to serve this corner of Stanhope, known as S. S. No. 3. The first was built of logs in 1866 farther south, closer to Boshkung Lake. (The transliteration of the Algonquian word meaning "Meeting of Three Waters" has gone through many transformations over the years. While the name of the lake is accepted as Boshkung, old-timers still refer to these four corners as Boskung. The "h" seems to have been added when the post office was established.)

The first school was burned down in 1874 or 1875, either by taxpayers angry about rising school taxes or by a lone man for unknown reasons. Whoever did it took care to remove the school's

This dingy building was the second school built to serve S.S. No. 3. It lasted from 1876 to 1905, when the third school was built at the four corners to the north. Photo courtesy Carol Moffatt.

Bible and place it on a stump out of reach of the flames before setting the building alight.

The second school was built in 1876 on land donated by Joseph Beatty on the rise south of the first school. The Methodists held their church services here until St. Stephen's was built in 1901 (see No. 11 above); in 1897, there were 52 youngsters enrolled in Sunday School.

The third school was built in 1905. It boasted a stone basement; over the years, a concrete floor, electricity, and indoor toilets were added. In 1939, students from S.S. No. 4 at Hall's Lake were sent here. In the mid-1960s, the school was sold into private hands. After standing empty for a few years, it became a residence.

13 · BUTTERMILK FALLS

Buttermilk Falls is one of the most dramatic watercourses in the county—and one of the most popular picnic spots. There have actually been three names given to this spot. An old postcard calls it White Horse Rapids. It was also said to have been called Davis Falls, after a logger who dropped his jug of buttermilk into the water—leading, naturally, to the name we now know it by.

The concrete structure that divides the upper part of the waterway was a log chute, built to replace an earlier wooden one.

Walk down the path beside the tumbling, roaring waters all the way to the outlet, where you can survey the length of Boshkung Lake.

The odd concrete abutment that runs down the upper part of Buttermilk Falls was a log chute. When the picture was taken for this postcard, the section closest to the camera was made of wood.

14 · FIRST STANHOPE COUNCIL CHAMBERS

This building was the first official home of the Stanhope Municipal Council. Before that, council meetings were held in homes. These chambers were built in 1910 and served the township until 1968, when the municipality took over the school farther along the road (see No.

98

15 below). The tiny building was also used for less solemn purposes, though. In the old days, it often rocked to the fiddling and foot-stomping of community square dances.

15 · BEECH LAKE SCHOOL

The Beech Lake School was built in the early 1920s. Industrious workers spelled out its official designation, S. S. (for School Section) No. 5, on the stairs in empty copper gunshells. The school became the municipal building for Stanhope Township in 1968. Since 1991, when the new township office was built just east of Highway 35, it has been a private residence.

16 · ANGLICAN RECTORY

This white house became the rectory for St. Peter's Anglican Church in 1915, when the church became the focal point of a charge that included St. Andrew's in West Guilford and St. Stephen's near Boskung. When the parishes were rearranged and St. Peter's was made part of the Haliburton charge, the minister moved there, and the rectory was sold in 1962 into private hands. St. Peter's is now part of the Minden charge.

17 · ST. PETER'S ANGLICAN CHURCH

St. Peter's is the work of John Henry Billing, the master stonemason who created a number of lovely buildings in this county. As a home for himself and his wife, Charity Wyatt, he built Blagdon Hill, named for the town in Somersetshire, England, where he was born in 1838. He built homes for his wife's three sisters, who had come with them from

St. Peter's Anglican Church was built in 1905 and 1906 by the congregation under the supervision of stonemason John Henry Billing. In 1910, he added the stone wall out front.

England and married local men (see the Cooper House above and the Sisson House below). He built the house called Lakeview in Haliburton village. And there are others. But the acknowledged masterpiece among all Billing's works is St. Peter's Anglican Church, Maple Lake.

The first church to stand on this site was a frame structure, which Billing had also had a hand in constructing when it was put up in the 1880s, around the time he arrived in the area. A stone tablet, now on the wall of the current church, was unveiled to commemorate the opening of the frame church on St. Peter's feast day, June 29, 1887.

Over the next decade or so, as the congregation grew, it was decided that a warmer and more substantial building was in order. The project finally got rolling in 1905, with Billing supervising the entire congregation in erecting the new church.

Two brothers, Eldon and Arthur Dawson, were his assistants. Pine lumber was donated by parishioners, planed at a nearby mill, and fashioned by local carpenters. The stone was collected from a nearby hill, and sand and gravel were brought from the river.

To make the mortar, William Welch burned limestone into lime at a kiln on the shore of Maple Lake. George Fader mixed the mortar. In 1967, at the age of 99, Fader was still alive to tell the tale. "Billing was a perfectionist," he said at that time. "Time meant nothing if the job was done right."

Billing and his helpers laboured from early spring until late October and on the next St. Peter's feast day—June 29, 1906—the new church was officially opened with a service of holy communion. Thanks to the contribution of labour by the men of the congregation and to the tireless activity of the women, who raised money with a bewildering variety of teas, suppers, concerts, and picnics, St. Peter's began its new lease on life debt-free.

In 1910, Billing added the matching stone wall that fronts the church. To keep people from sitting on it and contributing to its untimely disintegration, he put great globs of rough concrete along the top.

John Henry Billing was responsible for several fine stone buildings around the county. St. Peter's Anglican Church, Maple Lake, is acknowledged to be his masterpiece. Photo courtesy St. Peter's Anglican Church, Maple Lake.

Those are the main points of the story. But even this short a history of St. Peter's would be incomplete without mention of B. Napier Simpson. A Toronto-based architect and an expert in architectural conservation, Simpson bought Blagdon Hill from Billing's niece Charlotte

Cooper in 1957 and painstakingly restored it. Although the Simpsons continued to live in Toronto, they became such a part of the local community that, when he was killed in a plane crash in Newfoundland on June 23, 1978, Simpson was buried at St. Peter's. The family donated the stained-glass west window of the church in his memory. Blagdon Hill, on the high ground overlooking Maple Lake, Big Hawk Lake, and Little Hawk Lake, is still the Simpson family's summer home.

18 · SISSON HOUSE

Billing built this handsome stone farmhouse for his sister-in-law Anne Wyatt and her husband, Edward Sisson. Edward was better known throughout the community as Uncle Neddie and served as the postmaster for the area for a while, handling the mail from here. (Billing also built a house for his wife's third sister, Harriet Wyatt, who married John Hunt of Pine Lake, east of West Guilford.)

19 · CARNARVON SCHOOL

The first school on this site was a log building, set apart from other log schools by a front porch. The Methodist congregation of the district held services here until they built their own church in 1891 (see No. 2 above).

This school had a variety of names. It was called Brown's School because it stood on land donated by Andrew Brown. It was also known as the Union School because it brought together two school sections, S.S. No. 1 Stanhope and S.S. No. 10 Minden. In 1905, the log school was replaced with a frame building set about 80 feet farther back from the road. The school, which is now a private home, still sports its distinctive belfry.

DORSET VILLAGE

The view from the Dorset's highway bridge looks through the narrows, past the steep one-lane town bridge, and on to Trading Bay of Lake of Bays.

The village of Dorset began as Cedar Narrows, but long before the Europeans arrived, the Algonquians had cleared a few acres here to grow food. In addition to the usual crops of corn, beans, squash, and potatoes, these fields were famous for their sunflowerlike artichokes.

Isaac Hunter (see Chapter 9, No. 6) was the first white man known to have settled here. Whether he came this far in an effort to put as much distance as possible between himself and the long arm of the law after the Rebellion of 1837, or whether he genuinely preferred a reclusive life, the land he settled on at Hunter's Bridge on the Oxtongue River was his last stop. During one particularly harsh winter, he was found dead of starvation in his wilderness shanty. It is

said that his emaciated body was partly eaten by mice, which his second wife and his daughter were trying to catch to feed themselves.

In 1859, settler and trader Francis Harvey came to the area with his family. Said to have been one of the original surveyors of the Bobcaygeon Road, he had cleared a farm near Otter Lake. The Harveys later built a log cabin and a small trading post on the shore of Lake of Bays south of the narrows (behind the present Dorset Garage). Hence the name Trading Bay for the part of Lake of Bays west of the town.

In 1863, construction on the Bobcaygeon Road reached the Oxtongue River, just south of Dwight. (It was originally intended that the road would go to Lake Nipissing. Survey work was completed that far, but the Oxtongue River proved to be its northern terminus.) Settlers followed hard on the heels of the road-builders, and that year, 64 families were settled on the purportedly excellent farmland around Trading Bay.

Zachariah and Sarah Ann Cole were among those families. Zack Cole was a friend of Isaac Hunter. It was he who found the dead Hunter and his starving family. The Coles bought 17 acres on the north side of the narrows, where they built a house for themselves and a hotel to serve the loggers. In 1879, Cole drew up a survey of the area and changed the name of the community from Cedar Narrows to Colebridge. In 1883, when postal service began, the hamlet was renamed Dorset because there was already a town named Colebridge elsewhere in Canada.

Since the formation of the County of Haliburton in 1874, Dorset has been split down the middle by the line between Haliburton and the District of Muskoka. Wags like to say that if you fall off the town bridge and drown, which ambulance service comes to collect your body depends on which side of the bridge you fell off.

FROST CENTRE

The Leslie M. Frost Natural Resources Centre (7 1/2 miles south of Dorset) began in the 1940s as the Ontario Forestry School, a joint project of the University of Toronto and the provincial Department of Lands and Forests (now the Ministry of Natural Resources). The government used the facility to train forest rangers and conservation officers, and the university used it to provide practical training for its students in the Faculty of Forestry.

In 1966, the name was changed to the Ontario Forest Technical School; in 1969, the university gave up its lease on the surrounding forests and the facility became purely a training centre for government staff.

In 1971, discussion began about using the school as a base for broader outdoor education for the public, including schoolchildren. This move was supported by Leslie M. Frost, a former premier of Ontario and MPP for Victoria–Haliburton. On February 20, 1974, Premier Bill Davis named the centre in honour of Frost. The Frost Centre is now host to hundreds of school groups each year. Budget restraints have forced cuts in the wide range of programs offered to the general public in the summer, but the hope persists that they will be reintroduced one day.

Over the years, the staff of the Frost Centre have also developed a network of portages and campsites in the 18,000 acres of beautiful wilderness at its back door to make the area accessible to canoeists. Trails beginning near the centre are available for hiking in summer and cross-country skiing in winter.

GILMOUR TRAMWAY

A number of lumbering companies operated in the Dorset area in the decades leading up to the turn of the century: Langford Lumber, Rathburn, American Boom, J.D. Shier, and Mickle and Dyment, to name a few. One of the largest was the Gilmour Lumber Company, which had mills at Trenton on Lake Ontario.

In 1892, the Gilmours bought the cutting rights to about two-thirds of Peck Township, in Algonquin Park, for $1 million. But all the waterways to

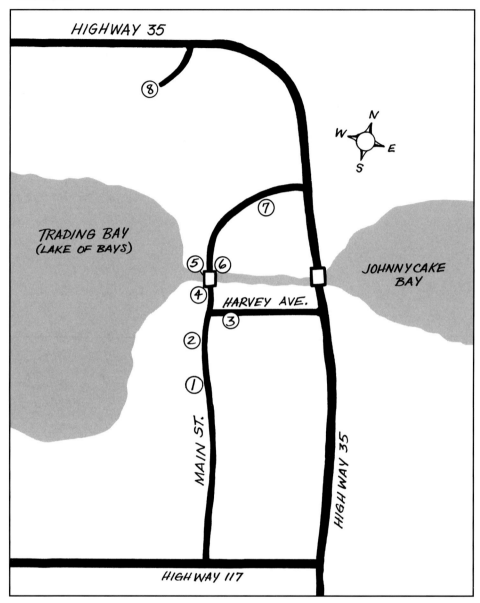

carry the logs led west to Muskoka and Georgian Bay, not south to Trenton.

Undaunted, the Gilmour brothers looked for a way to carry their logs over the height of land between the two watersheds. The result was the Gilmour Tramway, an undertaking that required two years, another million dollars, and the labour of a thousand men to build. By the spring of 1895, it was ready.

The logs travelled 20 miles from the park along the Oxtongue River to a steam pumphouse built of stone on the shore of Lake of Bays about a mile west of Dorset. Water was pumped up a wooden trough to ease the movement of the logs as they were lifted 80 feet up the trough by a jackladder to the top of the first grade. From here, they were floated down a timber sluiceway for about a mile to the start of the second jackladder; in some places, the sluiceway stood 30 feet in the air. Another series of pumps moved the logs up another trough to Raven Lake. The level of water in the lake had been raised so that it would flow into St. Nora's Lake at the top of the Trent River system.

Throughout the 1895 season, 1,500 logs a day were hoisted from one watershed to the other. The logs took three years to reach the mill at Trenton. By the time they arrived, they were unfit to cut. To add to the company's troubles, the demand for squared timbers had passed.

The bankruptcy of the Gilmour Company around 1910 put paid to the whole logging era as a significant economic force in Haliburton County. Eventually the timber sluiceway, abandoned and rotten, crumpled like a row of dominoes. The only thing left of the Gilmour Tramway today is the stone pumphouse, which has been turned into a cottage.

1·THE LOCKMAN HOUSE

The Lockman family were among Dorset's first settlers. Four girls and a boy were born to them at their farm on Otter Lake. As the children grew, however, the parents decided to move into town so that the youngsters could attend school. The lakeside property they bought from the Mickle and Dyment Lumber Company already boasted a building the company had used for an office and storage depot.

The Lockmans turned the building into a house, adding many improvements, including windows in the top storey, a kitchen in the back half, and spacious verandahs all around. Members of the Lockman family lived in the house until the early 1960s.

2·ST. MARY MAGDALENE ANGLICAN CHURCH

The story of St. Mary Magdalene Anglican Church officially began at a vestry meeting on April 28, 1894. Four months earlier, Frank Harvey had deeded a plot of land on a rise near the shore of Lake of Bays for the church site. Harvey and his wife were clearly generous people of an ecumenical stripe: that same year, they also donated the land for Knox Presbyterian Church, which stands around the corner on Harvey Avenue (see No. 3 below).

Just days less than a year later— on April 16, 1895—the congregation held its first services in the new building. Photographs on the wall at the back of the current church show it to have been a spare and simple structure. The priest was the Rev. Alexander William Hazlehurst, who was the priest at St. Ambrose Church in Baysville and had charge of St. Mary Magdalene from

1895 to 1927—an unusually long tenure for a rural clergyman at any time.

Hazlehurst made the trip from Baysville by boat in summer and horse and sleigh in winter. When weather conditions kept him home, Raymond Fisher, the local druggist, acted as lay reader. On those occasions when there was no service at St. Mary Magdalene, the congregation went around the corner to Knox Presbyterian.

The original church burned in 1907. Although no written record exists of the date of construction of the present building, it is generally agreed that it was erected in 1909 or 1910.

The church was served by priests resident in Baysville until 1941, when it was transferred to the Cowley Fathers in Bracebridge. The Cowley Fathers, members of the Society of St. John the Evangelist, are remembered with great affection as truly Christian people who came to Dorset any way they could get here—by foot, by bicycle, by boat.

In 1955, the Lake of Bays Mission was formed to include Baysville, Port Cunnington, Fox Point, and Dorset, where the new rectory was located. Until their monastery closed in 1983, however, the Cowley Fathers continued to fill in whenever the mission was between priests.

Naturally, with the clergy at such a distance, the health and strength of the congregation has rested in the hands of its members. Special credit is given to the Clayton family and to Phyllis Briscoe, who was church treasurer from 1966 to 1988 and organist from 1959 to 1989.

3 · KNOX UNITED CHURCH

Knox Presbyterian Church, the other church built on land donated by Frank Harvey and his wife, was erected in 1894. The lumber was cut at Angus Mackay's sawmill and the building was erected, as was customary, by community labour.

About 1914 or 1915, Basil Henry, the Presbyterian minister of the day, put his cabinetmaking skills to work and, with Erasmus Lockman, built a dozen new pews from lumber donated by Mackay. All the pew ends were sawn from a single birch log, the largest tree Mackay ever cut down.

The year 1925 brought church union: Methodist and Presbyterian congregations across the Dominion combined to form the United Church of Canada. (Dorset's Methodist church stood across the road from the Anglican church. It subsequently became first the Orange Hall and then a public school before it was demolished.) To celebrate church union and accommodate the larger congregation, 20 feet were added to the south end of Knox to form a chancel. The windows behind the altar are clear, unlike those in most churches, and offer a lovely view of the wooded ridge and the split-rail fence running behind the church.

At this time, a stone wall was built around the perimeter of the property by James Norrie of Norland. The two main slabs of native pink granite in the gate posts were not shaped to fit, but came from the ground as square as they stand now. The row of cedar trees Angus Mackay planted along the western property line after the wall was completed still thrives. Over the decades, however, the wall disintegrated badly. In 1994, to mark the church's centennial, the congregation restored the wall and dedicated it to the memory of Norm Mackay, a son of Angus Mackay and a lifelong church member who had died the year before.

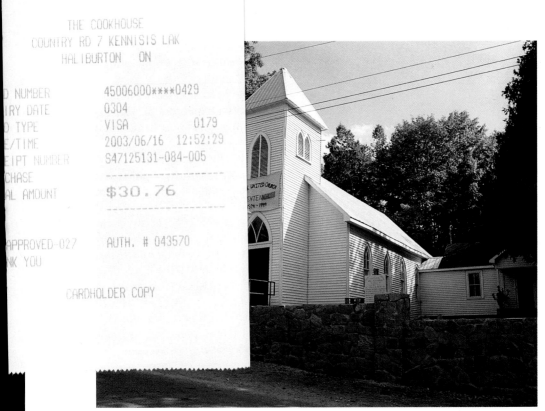

Knox United Church celebrated its centennial in 1994. The congregation marked the occasion by restoring the stone wall out front and dedicating it to the memory of Norm Mackay.

Except for the Sunday school wing added in the 1940s, Knox United remained unchanged from 1925 to 1985, when, to mark its 90th anniversary, the church was renovated—again by community labour. This time, the women of the church did much of the carpentry work, as well as stripping and varnishing the wood throughout, making cushions for the chancel chairs and pews, and donating the carpet.

Several artifacts found when the interior was taken apart have been preserved in a display case in the church. Among them is a Neilson's candy-bar wrapper that had slipped down between the cracks one day long ago. The Neilson family had had a cottage in the area and enjoyed a long connection with

the community and the church. Not only did they teach for years in the Sunday school, they also donated the first two electric organs to Knox United.

4 · CLAYTON'S STORE AND THE POST OFFICE

This store, on the Muskoka side of the road, was first opened by Thomas Ball in 1879. There were two other owners before Isaac Newton Langford took it over in 1891, when it also became the third location for the post office. In 1904, the post office was moved across the street to Frank Cassidy's store in Haliburton (where the municipal parking lot is now) until 1912, when it came back to Muskoka. By this time, the store on this side was owned by Edward Speers.

In 1879, Thomas Ball opened the first store on the site of the present Langford Landing.
Photo courtesy Irene Clayton.

The post office was still part of the store when it was bought in 1922 by David Wesley Clayton, son of Jeremiah Clayton, an Irish immigrant who had moved down from Fletcher Lake around 1905 to establish a trading post in the village. Clayton's Store became a fixture of Dorset life. David's son Jack took over both the store and the post office in 1964. In 1971, the present post office building was built on the other side of the road in Haliburton, and Jack continued to run both store and post office. Jack's son John took over Clayton's in 1980 and became postmaster in 1990.

In 1996, the Clayton family sold the property to the Blakes of Gravenhurst, who now operate it and the adjacent marina, cafe, and resort.

5 · THE TOWN BRIDGE

The original bridge that carried the Bobcaygeon Road across the narrows was intended to be temporary and was therefore built on a floating base. Zack Cole is said to have replaced it with a fixed wooden structure; perhaps that's what inspired him to change the name of the village from Cedar Narrows to Colebridge. In 1914, the Western Bridge and Equipment Company of Chatham, Ontario, was hired to replace the bridge. That year they put in a concrete base with a wooden top. The next year, they replaced the wooden portions with concrete. Years later, iron railings and a sidewalk were added.

Increasing traffic eventually made the steep, one-lane bridge more of an inconvenience than a curiosity. In 1957, the "highway" bridge was put in to carry the Highway 35 by-pass around the town. To accommodate it, some houses had to be moved; the house Angus Mackay had built, which still belonged to his family, was demolished.

6 · Robinson's General Store

Robinson's General Store stands on the site of Zack Cole's original Colebridge Hotel and trading post. After Cole's death, his property was sold to Fred McKey and his wife. McKey began the expansion of the store. After his death, McKey's widow, Marguerite, married Harry Robinson, and the name of the store changed for the last time. Since Harry's death in 1975, the store has been operated by his son Bradley. In 1981, Robinson's was voted Canada's Best Country Store.

Steamboats

From 1876 to about 1952, steamboats plied the lake between Huntsville and Dorset. Over the decades, there were nine steamboats: the *Waubamik*, the *Excelsior*, the *Equal Rights*, the *Nishka*, the *Maple Leaf*, the *Mary Louise*, the *Joe*, the *Mohawk Belle*, and the *Iroquois*.

In the first half of this century, the steamboats made two round trips a day between Huntsville and Dorset. The first trip left Dorset each day at six or seven in the morning and got back between

Steamboats ran on Lake of Bays between Huntsville and Dorset for over 75 years. In the first half of this century, they made two round trips a day, carrying passengers, freight, and mail. When the tourist traffic was in full swing, it seemed every boat was loaded. In this photograph, the Iroquois, *which ran from 1907 to 1948, is pulled up at the dock beside Clayton's Store. Photo courtesy Haliburton Highlands Museum.*

noon and one. Within the hour, the boat left again, returning between seven and nine in the evening. The crew did not sleep on the boat, but in part of the building that later became Clayton's Store. The first floor was for storage, the second for sleeping quarters. Most prominent of the several captains who served on the steamboats was Captain David Langford, the first captain of the *Iroquois*, which ran from 1907 to 1948. His name lives on in the Langford Canoe Company, located on the highway outside of town.

7 · DORSET SCHOOL

The first Dorset school was built in 1879 or 1880 by Francis Hoover at the head of Johnnycake Bay, the part of Lake of Bays east of town. This frame building was later moved to the foot of the "mountain" at the north edge of town and reestablished on land donated by Jeremiah Clayton. This site is now occupied by the Ministry of the Environment. The frame school was later replaced by a one-room brick building across the road on the present school site.

As the population swelled, two other buildings were also pressed into service: the Orange Lodge (which stood across from the Anglican church and had originally housed the Methodist church) and another building on the site of the current school. Classes were consolidated in 1961 in a new two-room brick building on the present site. Two more rooms and a library were subsequently added.

In 1986, the Board of Education wanted to close the school because of falling enrolment. The community rallied, however, and proved that the number of young couples living in the area would ensure rising enrolment in just a few years. As well, the parents of children then in the school did not want to subject their youngsters to long schoolbus rides. The community won the day, the Dorset school remained open, and the predictions of rising enrolment have come to pass.

The first lookout tower on the hill above Dorset provided an excellent vantage point for fire-rangers scanning the distant hills for telltale signs of forest fires. The present tower attracts sightseers.

8 · LOOKOUT TOWER

From its vantage point high on the hill above the town, the Dorset Tower affords a splendid view of the surrounding area. A fire-rangers' tower was built on this site—purchased from Jeremiah Clayton for $25—in 1922. Until 1961, when aircraft were introduced, fire-

Those willing to climb the 118 steps to the top of the Dorset Lookout Tower are rewarded with a spectacular view of more than 300 square miles of the surrounding countryside.

rangers spent their summer days up here, watching for fires in the surrounding hills.

In 1967, the original tower was replaced with the current structure, which was purchased by the Ministry of Natural Resources from the Department of National Defence and moved here.

There are 118 steps to the upper observation deck, 155 yards above lake level, which affords a view of 310 square miles. There is a park with picnic facilities at the base of the tower. Both the park and the tower are open from May 1 to Thanksgiving.

CHAPTER ELEVEN

OTHER WAYS TO EXPLORE HALIBURTON

STUDIO TOUR

Since it started in 1988, the Haliburton County Studio Tour has become one of the area's most successful events. Two dozen artists and artisans open their studios to the public, and some 2,000 people come to visit—and to buy. The work offered in the juried tour is of consistently high quality, whether it is painting, pottery, weaving, woodworking, sculpture, stained glass, jewellery, knitting, dolls, wicker furniture, or any of the other arts and crafts for sale.

The Haliburton County Studio Tour is held the weekend before Thanksgiving so that visitors can enjoy the splendid autumn colours as they drive around from studio to studio. Studio Tour maps are available beginning in June each year from the art galleries in Minden and Haliburton, the Chamber of Commerce Information Centre on Highway 35 at Minden, and several merchants throughout the county.

TRAILS

Haliburton County boasts 125 miles of snowmobile trails (along with the largest snowmobile club in the world) and 95 miles of cross-country ski trails. The hills of the Highlands make these trails among the most magnificent anywhere. The trails have been laid out to link the villages and resorts of the county. Lodge-to-lodge packages are available.

The railbed of the Victoria Railway from Kinmount to Haliburton village was bought by the county in 1988 to serve as a recreational trail. It makes a fine cycling and hiking trail in the snow-free seasons and an important thoroughfare for snowmobiling and other winter sports.

The Moose Wood Trail Centre on County Road 14 offers mountain biking, hiking, skiing, and snowshoeing (including rentals).

Trails have also been created by the Townships of Stanhope and Snowdon.

The Haliburton Forest and Wildlife Reserve, north of Kennisis, is a 50,000-acre private reserve that offers camping facilities, as well as an extensive network of trails for use in all seasons. Maps of these trails are available at the reserve.

Further information on and maps of trails in the Highlands are available at the Chamber of Commerce Information Centre on Highway 35 at Minden.

CANOE ROUTES

Exploring Haliburton by canoe is as easy as putting your boat in the water. To help you, the Ministry of Natural Resources has maps of the Gull River and Burnt River systems. There's also a cobweb of canoe routes in the lands managed by the Frost Centre. Maps of these portages and campsites are harder to come by, though, since they haven't been reprinted; a copy is available for study at the Frost Centre.

Kevin Callan's *Cottage Country Canoe Routes*, published by Boston Mills Press, shows some of the routes in the county. My own book *Water Ways: Exploring Haliburton by Canoe*, published by Kevker Publications in 1994, provides guided tours of 11 canoe trips in the Haliburton Highlands.

BIBLIOGRAPHY

All of these books except the ones marked by an asterisk are by past
or present residents of the Haliburton Highlands.

Bishop, Christopher. *Haliburton Highlands.* (Photographs). Introduction by J.
Douglas Hodgson. Self-published, 1989.

*Bennet, N.D., comp. *The Back Fifty.* Ontario Department of Highways, 1966.

*Brown, Ron. *Ghost Towns of Ontario.* Cannon Books. Vol. 1, 1992, Vol. 2, 1991.

Cummings, Harley R. *Early Days in Haliburton County.* Haliburton Highlands
Museum, 1993. (First printed in 1962 by Ontario Department of Lands and
Forests.)

Devitt, Ed H., and Nila Reynolds. *Echoes of the Past.* Self-published, 1980.

Dobrzensky, Leopolda z. Lobkowicz. *Fragments of a Dream: Pioneering in Dysart
Township and Haliburton Village.* Municipality of Dysart *et alii*, third edition 1992.

Dobrzensky, Leopolda z. Lobkowoicz. *They Worked and Prayed Together: Italians in
Haliburton County.* Self published, 1988.

*Guillet, Edwin C. *The Story of Canadian Roads.* University of Toronto Press,
1967.

Hone, Kenneth C. *Jacknives and Inkwells: A Rememberance of a One-Room
Schoolhouse in Haliburton County from 1954 to 1964.* Self-published, 1993.

Hulbig, John S. *Whispering Pines: A Haliburton Heritage.* Self-published, 1993.

Le Craw, F.V. *The Land Between.* Laxton, Digby, and Longford Council, 1967.

McEachern, Ruth, Kerry Greenaway, and Susan McKay. *Dorset Ontario.*
Herald-Gazette Press, Bracebridge, 1976.

Monmouth Historical Committee. *Monmouth Township 1881–1981: Collected
Views of the Past.* Township of Monmouth,1981.

*Murray, Florence B.ed. *Muskoka and Haliburton 1685 to 1850: A Collection of Documents*. Champlain Society, for the Government of Ontario, 1963.

Peacock, Theodore Roosevelt. *Tails of the Trail*. Glamorgan Township Centennial Issue, 1974.

Reynolds, Nila. *In Quest of Yesterday*. Provisional County of Haliburton, third edition 1973.

*Ryan, Lorna. "Ontario's Oldest Village–Minden" in *Canadian Motorist*, Vol. 20, No. 12, and Vol. 21, No. 1. Ontario Motor League, 1933 and 1934.

*Saunders, Audrey. *Algonquin Story*. Ontario Department of Lands and Forests, 1948.

Scott, Guy. *History of Kinmount: A Community on the Fringe*. Self-published, 1987.

Shirley, Michael. "Harnessing the Gull River" in *Minden and Area '87*. Kevker Publications. Minden, 1987.

Still, Ruth. *In the Fullness of Time: The Story of Eagle Lake*. Self-published, 1994.

Thompson, George S. *Up To Date or The Life of a Lumberman*. Self-published, 1895.

Wallace, Burleigh. *Haliburton Hills: Poems and Scenes of the Highlands*. Self-published, fourth edition 1970.

Wilkins, Taylor. *Haliburton by Rail and the I.B.&O.* Self-published, 1992.

INDEX

ACCOMMODATIONS

RESORTS & HOUSEKEEPING COTTAGES

Birch Point Lodge
A very traditional family resort; 75 years of proven customer satisfaction; 1,000 feet of safe, sandy beach; full American plan.
Dennis Casey
R. R. #2, Haliburton, Ontario K0M 1S0
Tel: 800-267-4429   705-457-2717
Fax: 705-457-1307

Bunny Hollo Cottages
Ten housekeeping cottages on 3.5 private acres just north of town; safe, sandy beach; lots of water activities; open May to October.
Chris and Eunice Lilly
P. O. Box 158, Dorset, Ontario P0A 1E0
Tel: 705-766-2491

* Chandler Point Lakeside Lodge
Keeping it simple, the way it used to be: seasonal housekeeping cottages and year-round lodge accommodation in a woodsy setting.
Hugh Taylor & Pamela Marsales
R. R. #2, Haliburton, Ontario K0M 1S0
Tel/Fax: 705-457-1671

Halimar Lodge
Traditional four-season family resort since 1950; standard-to-luxurious chalets, cottages, and suites in lodge; heated outdoor pool.
Angela & Jurgen Haedicke
R. R. #2, Haliburton, Ontario K0M 1S0
Tel: 800-223-7322   705-457-1300
Fax: 705-457-2559

* Hospitality Inn
Modern, heated, waterfront housekeeping cottages with a wide variety of up-to-date recreational facilities including swimming pool.
Al & Denise Leblanc
R. R. #1, Minden, Ontario K0M 2K0
Tel: 705-286-2361

Miners Bay Lodge
Specializing in relaxed, informal, family summer vacations since 1938; housekeeping cottages, cabins, rooms, trailer park; sports director.
Russ & Randy Wunker
R. R. #1 (Miners Bay)
Norland, Ontario K0M 2L0
Tel/Fax: 705-286-2978

Oldham's Inn
A turn-of-the-century country inn offering warm bed-and-breakfast hospitality and casual elegant dining. Fully licenced LLBO.
Vic & Carol Brown
R. R. #1 (Moore's Falls)
Norland, Ontario K0M 2L0
Tel: 705-454-8519   Fax: 705-454-9879

Ox Narrows Lodge
Historic 1935 log resort with housekeeping cabins, rooms, apts; licenced dining room, conv. store, gas, ice huts; at trails junction.
Diana Reesor
R. R. #2, Minden, Ontario K0M 2K0
Tel: 705-489-3885

* Ruby's Cottage Resort
Enjoy a relaxing summer vacation with your family at a traditional housekeeping cottage resort on beautiful Boshkung Lake.
Joanne and Bob Penfold
R. R. #2, Minden, Ontario K0M 2K0
Tel: 705-489-2193

Sandy Acres Resort
Four-season resort with housekeeping cottages on 2,000 feet of lakefront, plus tent campsites and new seasonal trailer park.
Laila and Andy Hillo
P. O. Box 88, Harcourt, Ontario K0L 1X0
Tel: 705-448-2372

* Sandy Lane Resort
Deluxe housekeeping waterfront chalets with fireplaces for hot days, snowy days, any day; hot tub under the stars; social centre.
Joachim Matysek
R. R. #2, Minden, Ontario K0M 2K0
Tel: 800-461-1422
Tel/Fax: 705-489-2020

Shadow Lake Resort
A place to relax for 50 years; renovated housekeeping cottages along a sandy beach; boat launch and marine services; plus new Gold Rock Cafe.
Harry and Penny Clasper
R. R. #1, Norland, Ontario K0M 2L0
Tel: 705-454-3242

* Shalom by the Lake
Four-season family resort with spacious housekeeping cottages; self-contained retreat centre accommodates 40; 300-foot sand beach.
Joe and Suzie Kegel
R. R. #2, Minden, Ontario K0M 2K0
Tel: 705-489-3674   Fax: 705-489-3163

* Silver Eagle Resort
Fourteen cosy four-season housekeeping cottages in a wooded waterfront valley, with children's playground, hot tub, rec. hall, and much more.
Marj & Larry
P. O. Box 157, Eagle Lake, Ontario K0M 1M0
Tel: 800-495-6348   705-754-2497
Fax: 705-754-1202

Silver Springs Cottages
Cosy, rustic, year-round housekeeping cottages with wood stoves, private showers/bathrooms. Sauna, private beach, docking facilities.
Lorne and Mary Coburn

* Establishments marked with an asterisk are shown on the map on the back cover.

P. O. Box 42, Harcourt, Ontario K0L 1X0
Tel/Fax: 705-448-2617

Sir Sam's Inn

Classic couples resort; superb food, secluded lakeside/ski-side setting; a variety of all-inclusive packages available year-round.
James Orr
P. O. Box 168, Eagle Lake, Ontario K0M 1M0
Tel: 800-361-2188   705-754-2188
Fax: 705-754-4262

Tall Pines

Cosy, clean, modern housekeeping cottages; beach and other low-key recreational facilities; western exposure; open May to October.
Ron & Cynthia Shorey
R. R. #2, Comp. 415
Minden, Ontario K0M 2K0
Tel: 705-489-4155

Trading Bay Inn

Eight housekeeping cottages on over 700 feet of waterfront; lots of docking; plus Rumors Cafe, Olde Clayton General Store, and marina.
Adrienne
P. O. Box 398, Dorset, Ontario P0A 1E0
Tel: 705-766-0783

Wigamog Inn Resort

Four-season classic country inn for families and couples; cottages with Jacuzzis, fireplaces; quality dining; waterfront; ski rentals.
Kimberley & Christopher Grossman
R. R. #2, Haliburton, Ontario K0M 1S0
Tel: 800-661-2010   705-457-2000
Fax: 705-457-1962
www.wigamoginn.ca/resort

* Willow Beach Cottages

Modern, family-oriented, self-catering, four-season cottages with fireplaces; sandy beach; central whirlpool, sauna, indoor recreational facilities.
Don & Marie Gage
R. R. #2, Haliburton, Ontario K0M 1S0
Tel: 800-656-9067   705-457-1110
Fax: 705-457-3189

* Woodland Cafe and Dance Hall

Sophisticated food and good music in a rustic lakefront setting; comfortable, eclectic atmosphere; limited accommodation available.
Lorna MacDougall
R. R. #2, Haliburton, Ontario K0M 1S0
Tel: 705-457-1892

Zum Waldhaus

Privacy and convenience year-round in a natural setting; housekeeping cottages; B&B in main house; tent/trailer sites; boats, trails, and more.
Dieter Dahlke
P. O. Box 46, Harcourt, Ontario K0L 1X0
Tel: 800-979-3486   705-448-2001
Fax: 705-448-1253

BED & BREAKFASTS

ALL-HART B&B

An historic lakeside year-round estate; luxurious rooms, all private ensuites, and guest lounge with Vermont fireplace.
Heather Alloway & Barry Hart
R. R. #2, Haliburton, Ontario K0M 1S0
Voice/Fax: 705-457-5272

Caleb's Meadow B&B

Family comfort in a renovated farmhouse; in-ground pool; full country breakfast; strolling distance to beach access, golf, etc.
Karen Saunders and David Snow
R. R. #2, Haliburton, Ontario K0M 1S0
Tel: 705-457-9486

Down Home B&B

Secluded in-town location within walking distance of the village and the lake; full breakfast and all amenities; smoke-free; no pets.
John and Cathy Down
P. O. Box 987, Haliburton, Ontario K0M 1S0
Tel: 705-457-4031

* House in the Village B&B

Estd. in 1905 by Clark ancestors, this former boarding house has offered homey lodgings to many travellers over the years.
Hilda Clark
P. O. Box 63, Wilberforce, Ontario K0L 3C0
Tel: 705-448-3161   705-448-2018

* Kinmount House B&B

A recently restored century home with an informal atmosphere and superb food; dinner and picnic lunches provided on request.
Patrick Healey
P. O. Box 33, Kinmount, Ontario K0M 2A0
Tel: 705-488-2421

Lakefront Cottage B&B

On the lake three km. from town; three rooms, private entry, spacious lounge and patio, swimming; full country breakfast; close to winter skiing.
Audrey and John Young
R. R. #2, Box 10, Haliburton, Ontario K0M 1S0
Tel/Fax: 705-457-5388

Lochside B&B

Friendly, comfortable, lakeside home; two queen bedrooms and one twin bedroom (wheelchair-accessible); full breakfast; no smoking; no pets.
Margaret and Martin Hill
P. O. Box 475, Haliburton, Ontario K0M 1S0
Tel: 705-457-9785

Minden House B&B

A gracious country home in town on the river; four bedrooms; full breakfast; plus five housekeeping cottages for family vacations.
Nora Snyder
P. O. Box 136, Minden, Ontario K0M 2K0
Tel: 705-286-4450

* Stone Hedge Farm B&B
350 secluded, picturesque acres, sandy beach, woods, meadows; B&B in homey century farmhouse or housekeeping in separate three-bedroom guest house.
Jim and Bernie Davis
R. R. #1, Minden, Ontario K0M 2K0
Tel: 705-286-1709   Fax: 705-286-4574

The Stone House B&B
Rustic elegance in secluded mature woods; full privacy, hearty gourmet breakfasts, walking trails through woods and wildflower meadows.
Phyllis Howarth
R. R. #3, Minden, Ontario K0M 2K0
Tel: 705-286-1250

Stouffer Mill B&B
A unique 12-sided home decorated with antiques on 130 acres; private decks and a rooftop solarium; full, hearty breakfast.
Don and Jessie Pflug
R. R. #2 (Hall's Lake)
Minden, Ontario K0M 2K0
Tel: 705-489-3024

* Sunny Rock Lodge B&B
"A magic oasis of relaxation, renewal, companionship, and peace" in a large historic 1928 Finnish-style log house (formerly a resort).
Sally Moore
R. R. #1 (Scott's Dam Road)
Minden, Ontario K0M 2K0
Tel: 705-286-4922   Tel/Fax: 416-759-5275

Sunnyside B&B
Three guest rooms in renovated 90-year-old farmhouse; walking distance to downtown, beach, and parks; smoke-free; breakfast of your choice.
Bonnie and Ken Cleeland
P. O. Box 235 (Sunnyside Street)
Haliburton, Ontario K0M 1S0
Tel: 705-457-9173
www.achilles.net/~bb/605.html

* Wild Swan B&B Inn
Casual elegance in a restored three-storey Victorian home in town on the river; private baths, Jacuzzis, gourmet breakfast, afternoon treats.
Paul and Linnea Baynton
P. O. Box 119, Minden, Ontario K0M 2K0
Tel: 705-286-3020
Call for 800 & fax numbers and e-mail address.

* Windrich Farm B&B
Fully restored 1874 log house sleeps four to six in four-season comfort and privacy; self-catering. B&B accommodations in main house.
Susan Orpana
R. R. #3, Comp. 300
Minden, Ontario K0M 2K0
Tel: 705-286-4984

TENT/TRAILER PARKS

* Jay Lake T&T Park
Seasonal sites, overnight camping, hard-floor tents

(some equipped for those with handicaps), private lake, pool, store.
Bernice and Jim Hollett
R. R. #1, Minden, Ontario K0M 2K0
Tel: 705-286-1233

Northern Eagle Tent and Trailer Resort
Family camping; daily, weekly, seasonal sites; options for permanent use; sandy beach; full service; washrooms, laundromat, store.
The Manager
R. R. #1, Minden, Ontario K0M 2K0
Tel/Fax: 705-286-2837

Pine Grove Point
Four-season trailer park, campground, winterized cottages; fishing, canoeing, snowmobiling, and more; opp. entrance to Algonquin Park.
Joe and Joy Danylyshen
P. O. Box 121, Harcourt, Ontario K0L 1X0
Tel: 705-448-2387

MOTELS

Bostonian Motel
Four year-round housekeeping units on the lake close to town; three-piece bathrooms with showers; paddle-boat rental.
Roberta and Max Walsh
P. O. Box 124, Wilberforce, Ontario K0L 3C0
Tel: 705-448-2185

Noble Motel & Restaurant
Year-round accommodation with licenced dining room and patio overlooking lake; sand beach, equipment rentals, and more.
Bob and Rose Thompson
R. R. #1 (Moore's Falls)
Norland, Ontario K0M 2L0
Tel: 888-286-6253   Tel/Fax: 705-454-8298

Nordic Inn
Ten spacious, first-class rooms; licenced dining room; 23 km. of own trails for hiking and cross-country skiing; open all year; near town.
Ben Minns
P. O. Box 155, Dorset, Ontario P0A 1E0
Tel: 705-766-2343   Fax: 705-766-9983

Silver Maple Motel
Comfortable units with three-piece baths, cable, air-cond; easy walking to shops, restaurants, beach, park; close to winter trails.
Gerry and Joan Irish
P. O. Box 365, Haliburton, Ontario K0M 1S0
Tel: 705-457-2607

Wagon Wheel Motel & Restaurant
Serving the Highlands for over 50 years; fully licenced; lovely pine decor, antiques; some rooms with Jacuzzi and fireplace; open all year.
Mark Steffensen
R. R. #3, Minden, Ontario K0M 2K0
Tel: 705-286-4122